The Service Culture Handbook

The Service Culture Handbook

A STEP-BY-STEP GUIDE TO GETTING
YOUR EMPLOYEES OBSESSED
WITH CUSTOMER SERVICE

● ● ●

Jeff Toister

ISBN-13: 9780692842003
ISBN-10: 0692842004

Table of Contents

Acknowledgements

● ● ●

My first book, *Service Failure*, was published in October 2012. People almost immediately started asking me when I would write another.

I resented that question at first. It's hard enough to write one book and I couldn't believe people were already talking about book number two. Now, I appreciate all the people who asked the question. It showed they saw something that I didn't—I had another book to write.

Michelle Burke and Adriana Perez are fantastic friends who helped make this book possible in a roundabout way. They connected me with representatives of the online training video company lynda.com (now LinkedIn Learning) at a trade show in 2013. One thing led to another, and I was suddenly making customer service training videos.

My very first video was filmed in August 2013 and formed the seeds for this book. It's called *Leading a Customer-Centric Culture*, and it outlined what elite companies do to get employees obsessed with service. (Check it out at www.lynda.com/JeffToister. You'll need a lynda.com account to view the course, but you can get a 10-day trial at www.lynda.com/trial/JeffToister.)

Finally, I owe my wife, Sally, an endless amount of gratitude. Her encouragement continuously inspires me to write.

Introduction

● ● ●

Tony D'Aiuto wanted to create an unforgettable experience.

He's an Airport Operations Center manager at the Tampa International Airport. Small children often lose a favorite stuffed animal while traveling through an airport, so D'Aiuto's goal was to reunite a child with a lost toy in a fun and unique way.

His plan was to take photos of the toy in various places around the airport to make it look like the stuffed animal had gone on a big adventure. He would then return the toy to the child along with photographs of its journey. D'Aiuto asked a colleague who oversaw the airport's lost and found department to alert him the next time a child lost a stuffed animal.

Once the plan was in place, he waited. And waited. It took two months for it to happen. D'Aiuto was ready when he finally got the call.

A six-year-old boy had lost his stuffed tiger, Hobbes. The boy and his Tampa-based family had already boarded their outbound flight when Hobbes was found, so it was too late to return it to them that day. D'Aiuto jumped into action.

"Being a hobbyist photographer, I thought I could have some fun and creativity with the ways I took photos of Hobbes's adventure during my lunch break," said D'Aiuto. He enlisted help from various people around the airport to photograph Hobbes with airport firefighters, riding on a luggage cart, by the airport control tower, and elsewhere.

D'Aiuto took his photos to Walgreens, where he used a coupon he had saved to make a hardbound photo book documenting Hobbes's adventure.

He then brought Hobbes and the photo book to the airport's lost and found department, so the family could retrieve them when they returned from their trip.

The family had been told that the boy's stuffed animal was waiting for them at the airport's lost and found. They headed there immediately after their flight landed, eager to reunite Hobbes with their son. It was a touching reunion, and the boy really enjoyed seeing the pictures of Hobbes on his great adventure. D'Aiuto's initiative had taken the traumatic experience of losing a favorite toy and turned it into something positive and fun. The boy's mother was moved to tears at the kindness displayed by D'Aiuto and the rest of the Tampa Airport staff.

The heartwarming story attracted national media attention. It was picked up by news outlets such as NPR, CNN, and *USA Today*.

You just don't hear customer service stories like this very often.

There are plenty of stories about service failures. Every week, there seems to be yet another company featured in a news story about shockingly poor service. Customer service leaders privately tell me they struggle simply to get their employees to consistently deliver basics such as courtesy, promptness, and helpfulness.

Why are the stories about outstanding customer service so rare?

It's not due to a lack of ideas. Bookstores are well stocked with books explaining how to provide outstanding customer service. Some describe how companies can create successful service strategies, while others provide tips and tactics for customer-facing employees.

There are many other places where you can find customer service ideas. There are conferences, motivational speakers, and seminars galore. Consultants like me write blog posts, record podcasts, and create videos. Nearly every customer service professional has attended a customer service training class at some point during their career.

The stuffed animal photo adventure certainly isn't a new concept. D'Aiuto got the idea after reading a similar story about a child who lost a stuffed lion at a museum in London, England. It's also been done by a museum in Canada, and a Ritz-Carlton in Florida did the same thing with a stuffed giraffe in

2012. The original concept may have come from a story about a lawn gnome that was stolen from a garden in the mid-1980s and returned to its owner with a photo album depicting its various adventures. Or it may have originated from a popular children's book called *Flat Stanley*, which was published in 1964.

I asked D'Aiuto why he went to so much trouble on his own time just to create a memorable experience for one child. "Tampa International Airport has a long history of being very people-focused, as opposed to plane-focused," he told me. He explained that everyone in the airport, from the CEO on down, is committed to providing exceptional service. "Our CEO, Joe Lopano, sets the tone for being efficient and hard-working, but he also fosters a sense of creativity and fun at the airport which makes employees feel comfortable enough to take a chance like I did with this little boy's lost tiger."

That's the real secret that explains why these types of stories are so rare: Tampa International Airport has done something that few organizations achieve. The airport has created an environment where employees are constantly thinking about outstanding service. They proactively look for ways to make a difference in their customers' lives, even if it means going far beyond their regular responsibilities. Employees prioritize passengers over planes, recognizing that airport operations are really just a means to help travelers get to wherever they're trying to go. Perhaps that's why the airport is consistently rated one of the best in the U.S. in Condé Nast's annual reader's poll.

In short, employees there are obsessed with service.

The Service Culture Handbook shows you how to create a customer-focused culture where employees in your organization are obsessed with service. It's a step-by-step guide to help customer service teams, business units, and even entire companies get excited about serving customers at the highest level.

You'll get an inside look at companies—like REI, JetBlue Airlines, and Publix—that consistently rank near the top of their industries for customer service. You'll also find profiles of some lesser-known companies that represent the next wave of legendary customer service organizations. This book will show you what these elite organizations do that most organizations don't.

The Service Culture Handbook is organized into three parts. The first part examines why creating a customer-focused culture is the key to outstanding customer service. It also offers some cautionary tales about companies whose culture initiatives failed.

The second part provides detailed instructions for building a customer-focused culture. When you use these chapters to clearly define your organization's unique culture, you'll transform the way your employees view service. The ultimate goal is to get your employees obsessed with consistently delivering service that's so amazing it becomes part of your company's brand image.

Finally, the third part of the book helps you embed customer focus in your company's DNA, so you can sustain the customer-focused culture you've created. Companies that get really good at service will tell you they have to work at it every day. It's easy to grow weary or lose focus when you've worked long and hard at achieving a goal. These chapters assist you in keeping your employees engaged and making outstanding service the way that your company, department, or team simply does business.

Many chapters contain sample worksheets to help you implement these concepts. You can download blank copies of the worksheets from this book at www.serviceculturebook.com/tools. You'll also find additional tools and resources on the website, such as access to my Customer Service Tip of the Week email. You and your employees can sign up for these tips for free.

I recommend that you read each chapter in order, to get a clear picture of what it takes to create a customer-focused culture. You may be tempted to pick and choose lessons from this book. Please don't. This is a complete recipe for building a customer service culture. Just as you wouldn't try to bake a cake without flour or eggs, you shouldn't try to transform your organization's customer service while leaving out an essential ingredient. Also, it's a good idea to know exactly what you're getting into before you launch a major initiative.

I won't lie to you. Getting your employees obsessed with customer service is not easy. It is, however, one of the elements that separates the elite organizations from the rest. These companies put in the hard work that most aren't willing to dedicate themselves to.

Don't be afraid to use me as a resource as you explore these concepts. I'm easy to get in touch with:

Call or text: 619-955-7946

Email: jeff@toistersolutions.com

Twitter: @toister

You'll also find additional analysis, tips, and trends to help you develop a customer-focused organization on my *Inside Customer Service* blog at www.insidecustomerservice.com.

For now, I encourage you to turn to Chapter 1, where you'll read about another company whose employees are obsessed with customer service. In fact, these employees are so customer-focused that they did something that practically no one else would be willing to do.

Part 1: Culture Is the Key to Outstanding Customer Service

● ● ●

How Corporate Culture Guides Your Employees' Actions

● ● ●

THE INTERNAL NETWORK AT RACKSPACE went down and took the phone system with it. Customers suddenly weren't able to call. Employees couldn't even access the company directory to contact each other.

This was a potential disaster.

Rackspace provides computer hosting services for more than 300,000 customers. These companies run their websites, email, and internal computer systems on its network. It's all mission-critical stuff. When there's a problem, Rackspace customers need help fast.

A lone technical support agent sprang into action. He tweeted his personal phone number, letting customers know they could reach him directly if they needed help. Soon other tech support reps followed suit and tweeted their numbers, too. For the next four hours, they used Twitter and their cell phones to serve customers until Rackspace restored its phone service. The support team typically handles a thousand calls during a four-hour time frame, so their extraordinary service prevented a lot of unhappy customers.

The stakes were high, but nobody from management told these employees to tweet their personal phone numbers. It wasn't part of a carefully scripted procedure. No one even asked permission. They just did it.

HOW CULTURE CREATES HERO MOMENTS

Imagine the same scenario at nearly any other company. Employees would feel helpless. A few might lobby their supervisor to go home early. Most would just sit around and wait for the phone system to come back up.

The corporate communications department might post a message on the company's website to let customers know the phones were down. Somebody might tweet an update on the status of the phone system. That would likely be the extent of the company's efforts to alert customers to the problem.

Tweeting personal contact information would be unthinkable. Many customer service employees are fearful of giving out their last names, let alone their phone numbers. Employees at the average company would never take the kind of initiative that happened at Rackspace.

Rackspace isn't the average company, though. Stories of employees delivering over-the-top service are common. One rep ordered a pizza for a customer during a marathon trouble shooting session after she heard him mention that he was getting hungry. An account manager showed her appreciation for a visiting client by preparing a home-cooked meal.

The big question is why employees at Rackspace serve their customers in a way that's so different from the norm. It's too simplistic to say that Rackspace has made a company-wide commitment to provide outstanding service. Lots of companies make similar claims, but that doesn't mean they actually do it.

Their exceptional service isn't just a product of great training, either. Training works when you want to show someone how to use a specific skill or follow a particular procedure. Tweeting personal phone numbers, ordering pizza for a customer, and preparing a home-cooked meal for a client were all improvised moves. These actions were neither trained nor scripted.

The real secret to Rackspace's extraordinary service is their customer-focused culture. Employees are absolutely obsessed with taking care of their customers. They have created a unique identity, calling themselves Rackers, symbolizing the pride employees have in their company. They've developed a special brand of customer service called Fanatical Support® that promises customers they'll spring into action and do whatever it takes to help resolve any issue.

It's this obsession that leads to customer service hero moments like tweeting a personal phone number so customers can reach you.

A hero moment occurs any time an employee, a team, or an entire company rises to the occasion to provide customers with outstanding service. Hero moments aren't limited to over-the-top actions. They include everyday service encounters as well. In his book, *Be Your Customer's Hero*, customer experience strategist Adam Toporek defines it this way[1]:

> "It means being there when the customer needs you and making your personal interaction with the customer as memorably positive as possible."

Let's face it: the vast majority of customer-service interactions are unremarkable. They're neither amazingly good nor frustratingly bad. Think about the last time you went to the bank, bought a cup of coffee, or ordered something online. There's a good chance that nothing particularly extraordinary happened. It was business as usual.

A few experiences do stand out. We certainly remember the service failures. But we also remember the hero moments. Maybe you remember a kind bank teller who helped you avoid a fee. Perhaps there's a barista at your local coffee shop who makes you feel special every time he's there because he knows your name and your favorite drink. Or there may have been a time when you were shipped the wrong item, but the friendly customer service rep made the resolution so easy that you vowed to become a customer for life.

Every customer interaction is an opportunity for a hero moment or a service failure. Some businesses, like hotels, might have multiple interactions per day with the same customers. According to the Cornell Center for Hospitality Research, an average 250-room hotel has 5,000 daily guest interactions with valets, door people, bell staff, reception, restaurants, housekeeping, engineering, and other functions.[2]

The largest businesses might serve millions of customers on a daily basis. For example, Domino's Pizza delivers more than one million pizzas per day, seven days a week. Imagine all the customer service interactions required to make that happen! About 500,000 of those orders are taken by an employee (the rest are taken electronically, via their website, smart phone app, etc.). Employees must also deliver those one million pizzas. That means Domino's averages about 1.5 million hero or failure opportunities every day.[3]

Individual employees at some companies might personally serve dozens of customers per day. For example:

* A typical airline flight might have 150 passengers served by four flight attendants.
* A retail cashier might serve 20 customers (or more) per hour.
* A contact center agent might serve 10 (or more) customers per hour.

It's impossible for a boss, a policy, or a system to control all these interactions. Employees must exercise independent discretion at times. This is a scary reality for customer-service leaders, who worry their employees will do something wrong.

I've spoken to thousands of customer service employees over the years. Most want to do a good job and make their customers happy. The vast majority of these employees know how to deliver a hero moment, but they aren't actively looking for them. Sometimes the moment arises, but the employee doesn't feel empowered to spring into action. These are situations where the right corporate culture can encourage employees to make good decisions.

Culture creates hero moments on an individual level, where an employee strives to deliver the best customer service possible. That employee feels empowered to do what it takes to makes customers happy and takes pride in the company he or she works for. You see it in the way the employee greets customers, solves problems, and goes the extra mile when the situation demands it.

Culture also creates hero moments on a team level, where a department works together to serve its customers at a consistently high level. Team members share a passion for service that's absolutely contagious. You see it in their pervasive can-do attitudes and in the way they support each other in a collective effort to make their customers happy. These employees take pride in their team, yet always push each other to do even better.

Culture can create hero moments on an organizational level, as well, where an entire company is dedicated to providing outstanding service. Strategy, goals, policy, and other corporate decisions are made with the customer in mind. You see the impact of this customer focus in the legions of loyal customers who go out of their way to do business with these select companies.

It's no wonder that culture is such a hot topic in customer service. So, what exactly is it?

The Definition of Corporate Culture

Corporate culture can be a nebulous subject. There's a lot that goes into it, like mission, vision, and value statements. But while those are some of its elements, a company's culture is broader than that.

I turned to Catherine Mattice to get a clear definition. She's a consultant and trainer who specializes in helping organizations create a positive workplace culture. She's also the author of *Back Off! Your Kick-Ass Guide to Ending Bullying at Work,* and her research on the topic has made her an in-demand speaker at human resources conferences. Mattice has even served as an expert witness in court cases where corporate culture was a factor.

We met for coffee on a warm, sunny day. The coffee shop had a patio with just enough shade to make it comfortable. I thought it might be a short conversation, but we ended up talking for several hours.

We discovered that the challenge in defining culture is that there are so many valid perspectives. When Mattice helps companies end workplace bullying, she does so by focusing on their culture. I, too, focus on culture when I work with companies to help improve customer service. And when another colleague helps companies with their branding, she begins her efforts by focusing on their corporate culture, as well. It seems that so many things companies do can be boiled down to their culture.

Mattice and I agreed that while corporate culture can refer to an entire organization, it can also refer to a business unit, location, or individual team. It's not unusual for groups in different parts of a company to share some common characteristics, yet also have their own unique identity. You can't easily change the entire corporate culture if you're a store manager for a retail chain, but you can influence the culture within your particular store.

Mattice shared this definition, which puts it all together:

"Corporate culture is the way an organization's members think, act, and understand the world around them."

Let's use Rackspace as an example. Rackers certainly think, act, and understand the world around them differently than employees at most companies. When faced with an unexpected challenge, such as the phones going down, Rackers think, "My customers need me. I have to find a way to help them." They act to do something about it. Rackers do this because they understand how critical their services are to their clients' businesses.

Contrast this to the customer service most of us receive every day. Many employees think about their job solely in terms of their assigned responsibilities. They act in accordance with company policies and procedures, but rarely take initiative. They understand their role, but may not understand the company's goals. Or, employees might understand the company's goals, but not care about helping to achieve them.

All organizations have a culture. It doesn't have to be something intentionally created. In most organizations, culture organically develops over time through corporate strategy, the decisions of its leaders, the way employees interact with each other, and many other factors.

It's natural for a group of people to develop a certain amount of collective thinking. When you hear people say, "That's how we do things around here," they're referring to their company's culture. A few elite companies, like Rackspace, intentionally strive to cultivate a positive, customer-focused culture.

That intentionality is what's missing in many organizations. According to Mattice, most companies have policies that tell employees what they *should not do*. Companies with positive cultures help employees understand what they *should do*. Mattice explains that without clear guidance, "People don't know how else to act."

But you can't tell employees specifically what to do in every situation; there are too many variables. Instead, an intentionally-guided culture acts as a compass that consistently points employees in the right direction. That culture is reinforced when employees encounter a hero moment and make the right decision.

INSIDE RACKSPACE'S CUSTOMER-FOCUSED CULTURE

Rob La Gesse is the Vice President of Social Strategy at Rackspace. Most corporate executives in publicly traded companies are hard to contact. Not La Gesse. I got his phone number when he sent it to me via Twitter.

I asked La Gesse why he shares this information so freely. His explanation was simple: "I'm in the people business. I want people to find me."

He's not kidding. La Gesse published his cell and home phone numbers on his blog in 2009. It was 2013 when the Rackspace technical support rep tweeted his own cell number in order to be accessible to customers in need. Sharing a personal phone number via social media wasn't a scripted move, but it was embedded in the company's organizational thinking and exemplified by its leaders.

Accessibility is just one illustration of how Rackspace creates a customer-focused culture. Another is how it hires employees. According to La Gesse, the company hires many people who don't have technical backgrounds. They come from hospitality, medical, and similar professions that attract people with natural empathy.

La Gesse shares an example of the type of people they like to hire at Rackspace. He was attending an offsite meeting at a hotel. The meeting ended for the day, and the attendees headed off to the hotel's bar. There were only three bartenders, who were working like crazy to keep up.

La Gesse ordered a frozen margarita but received a margarita on the rocks. He was deep in conversation with a colleague and saw the long line at the bar, so he decided not to bother with getting his order corrected.

A few minutes later, the bartender approached La Gesse with a frozen margarita. He apologized for the error and told La Gesse that both drinks were on the house.

La Gesse was impressed. Mistakes can and will happen, especially during busy times. But it takes a special kind of person to recognize their mistake and go out of their way to fix it when the customer hadn't complained.

He waited for the bar to calm down a bit and then approached the bartender. La Gesse handed him his business card and said, "You need to be a Racker." The bartender was eventually hired by Rackspace. Although he had no experience working with computer networks, he turned out to be a perfect fit. He now has a successful career in technical sales.

"I can teach anybody [the computer operating system] Linux," said La Gesse. "I can't teach them to actually care."

Rackspace specifically looks for people like this, who fit the company's customer-focused culture. Here's a passage from its Fanatical Support Promise:

> *We cannot promise that hardware won't break, that software won't fail, or that we will always be perfect. What we can promise is that if something goes wrong, we will rise to the occasion, take action, and help resolve the issue.*

This isn't just something that's tucked into an employee handbook and then forgotten. This promise is a way of doing business at Rackspace. It's how Rackers think, from executive leadership all the way to the employees on the front lines of customer service.[4]

Fanatical Support is the first of the company's six core values:

1. *Fanatical Support® in all we do.*
2. *Results first. Substance over flash.*
3. *Treat Rackers like friends & family.*
4. *Passion for our work.*
5. *Full disclosure & transparency.*
6. *Committed to greatness.*

What truly makes these values special is that they're ingrained in hiring, training, and all aspects of guiding the employees' work. The company even has a "Culture" page on its website to explain it all:[5]

"Our Core Values came from us, the employees. They are our collective thoughts and beliefs encompassed by six values. Our leadership had no input or vote in them. We wouldn't even let them spell check our values. Luckily for us, our bosses are smart enough to know that telling employees what to think and believe is a complete waste of time, and just a bad idea all the way around."

These values truly represent how Rackspace does business. You see this in an employee tweeting his cell phone number to be accessible to customers in need. You see it in a bartender who gets hired after going out of his way to fix a drink order. In fact, you see examples of Fanatical Support® reinforced every single day at Rackspace.

"You have to constantly work at it," said La Gesse. "You have to constantly talk about."

The Dark Side of Corporate Culture

What leaders constantly work at and talk about has a profound impact on a company's culture. It shapes how employees think about, act upon, and understand service. Focus on the wrong things, and a company can unintentionally develop an anti-customer culture.

Comcast provides a clear warning. It's generally considered to have some of the worst customer service in the country. It was rated the worst internet service provider in the United States by the 2015 American Customer Satisfaction Index, and third and fourth worst respectively in subscription television and phone service.[6] Comcast also ranked dead last in the 2015 Temkin Customer Service Ratings.[7]

Comcast has been known to attract national media attention with its epic service failures. One particular example happened in July 2014. A Comcast subscriber named Ryan Block called to cancel his service. The customer service agent inexplicably stonewalled his request. Block was ten minutes into the call when he decided to record it.[8]

The recording lasts for approximately eight minutes. On it, you can hear the Comcast employee repeatedly badgering Block about his decision to cancel. Block politely asked the agent to cancel his service multiple times, but the employee continuously tried to talk him into retaining his account.

Block posted the recording online and it quickly went viral. Major news outlets reported on it. Tom Karinshak, Comcast's Senior Vice President of Customer Experience, issued a statement apologizing for the incident:

> "We are very embarrassed by the way our employee spoke with Mr. Block and are contacting him to personally apologize. The way in which our representative communicated with him is unacceptable and not consistent with how we train our customer service representatives."[9]

It's convenient for companies like Comcast to blame a rogue employee for an embarrassing service failure like this. However, a closer look reveals that the employee's actions were completely reflective of Comcast's corporate culture.

Canceling an account with Comcast in July 2014 was a difficult task. The instructions weren't easy to find on its website. Even searching "cancel account" failed to point customers to the desired result.

Customers who did find the cancellation instructions were instructed to call customer support. They could do almost anything online, including adding services, but Comcast wanted them to call to cancel.

Customers who called to cancel their accounts were transferred to someone called a "Retention Specialist." These employees were given training on step-by-step procedures they were expected to use to discourage customers from canceling. They received a bonus based on how many customers they could talk out of canceling their service. The employees received no bonus if too many customers insisted on canceling anyway.

The Retention Specialist on Ryan Block's recorded call summarized the role perfectly. He said, "My job is to have a conversation with you about keeping your service."

Comcast designed its entire cancellation process around trying to convince customers not to cancel. This philosophy was embedded in its process, and it was integrated into employee compensation. Retention was what these employees worked at and talked about.

It's not hard to understand why Comcast is infamous for its poor service. Let's go back to Catherine Mattice's definition of corporate culture: the way a company thinks, acts, and understands the world around them. Comcast thinks about its customers in terms of revenue. It acts to do whatever it can to retain or increase that revenue in the short term. It understands that a lost account equals lost revenue. None of this focuses on serving customers.

In an interesting twist to the story, Comcast announced in May 2015 that it was implementing a multi-year plan to create a new corporate culture focusing on exceeding customers' expectations. It seems that even Comcast, at some level, understands the importance of having a customer-focused culture.

Comcast is hardly the only company whose actions create a culture of poor customer service. In my first book, *Service Failure*, I uncovered many examples of how a company's culture can lead to poor service.

In one story, a hotel associate deliberately provided her guests with poor customer service because she was afraid of being ostracized by her co-workers if she went out of her way to be helpful. The hotel's poor culture made it uncomfortable for her to provide great service.

Another story involved a bank employee who signed off on 400 home foreclosures per day without actually verifying that the homes met the criteria for foreclosure. He never stopped to consider the customers who owned those homes because the bank had a culture that encouraged employees to follow its procedures without question.

A customer service representative at yet another company told me he routinely lied to customers because he was instructed to do so by management. He had recently gotten this job after being out of work for a long time, and he was worried that he'd be out of work again if he didn't comply with management's directives. The company's leaders created a culture of fear, intimidation, and dishonesty.

I discovered something else while researching these stories. We would like to believe that we wouldn't act the way those people did if we were placed in a similar situation. The truth is, most of us would.

We naturally take behavioral cues from the people around us. Some are conscious, like the customer service employee who lied to customers so he could keep his job. Others are unconscious, like the bank employee who mindlessly signed off on home foreclosures. They're both examples of corporate culture at work.

GETTING CULTURE TO GUIDE EMPLOYEES' ACTIONS

People see how employees are obsessed with customer service in a company like Rackspace and think, "Of course! That's how it should be!" That's what makes creating a customer-focused culture so maddeningly difficult. It seems like it should be easy, but it isn't.

The challenge is that culture isn't attributable to just one thing. There's no single initiative that will magically get your employees to consistently make customer service a priority. Culture is the sum of all the things we do in an organization.

Here are just a few examples of questions whose answers influence how culture shapes employee behavior:

- Are employees given clear guidance on the company's culture, or are they expected to just figure it out?
- Are employees invited to help shape the culture, or are they disengaged?
- Are strategic decisions driven by culture, or are they made without regard for customers?
- Are goals and metrics aligned with the culture, or do they encourage shortcuts?
- Are business processes customer-focused, or do they put employees in awkward situations?
- Are employees empowered to deliver outstanding service, or are they constrained?
- Do leaders reinforce the desired culture, or do they contradict it?

Addressing these questions isn't easy. It takes time, energy, and resources. Building a customer-focused culture is a never-ending journey that tests the entire organization's commitment and dedication.

So before showing you how to build a customer-focused culture in your company, I've written the next chapter to explain why so many customer service culture initiatives fail.

NOTES:

1 Adam Toporek, *Be Your Customer's Hero* (New York: AMACOM, 2015).

2 Barbara M. Talbot, "The Power of Personal Service: Why It Matters, What Makes It Possible, How It Creates Competitive Advantage," *CHR Industry Perspectives,* no. 1 (September 2006).

3 "Facts and figures," *Domino's Pizza.* https://biz.dominos.com/web/about-dominos-pizza/fun-facts.

4 The full text of the Rackspace Fanatical Support® Promise can be found on the company website: http://www.rackspace.com/managed-hosting-support/promise.

5 Learn more about the Rackspace culture here: http://www.rackspace.com/talent/culture.

6 The American Customer Satisfaction Index publishes annual ratings for Comcast and many of its major competitors on its website: http://www.theacsi.org.

7 The Temkin Group publishes annual customer satisfaction ratings on its website: http://www.temkinratings.com.

8 Ryan Block. "Ryan Block's recorded cancellation phone call with Comcast." SoundCloud. https://soundcloud.com/ryan-block-10/comcastic-service.

9 Tom Karinshak, "Comcast Statement Regarding Customer Service Call," *ComcastVoices* (July 15, 2014).

CHAPTER 2

Why Culture Initiatives Often Fail

● ● ●

"I want us to be like the Apple Store."

That's how a Chief Information Officer (CIO) described the goal for his customer service project. He worked for a company that provided software and information services to corporate clients around the globe. He managed several internal departments, including a help-desk team supporting the computing needs for several thousand employees spread across six continents.

The company had an internal customer service survey, and his help desk wasn't scoring well. There had even been complaints about service quality from other executives. The CIO decided he needed to change the culture, and he wanted to get his employees obsessed about providing the type of outstanding customer service the Apple Store was known for.

He called me to ask for help. We talked about his situation, and I pressed him for more details about his vision. "What is it about the Apple Store that you want your team to emulate?"

There was a brief silence as the CIO thought. Finally, he said, "I like the Apple Store because they're good at customer service."

That was the best description he could muster. The problem was that the Apple Store and his company's internal help desk operations were so different that the comparison made little sense. There was no similarity other than their focus on computers.

The Apple Store is a gleaming showcase for Apple's latest technology. Employees are there to educate customers, help them find solutions, and sell products. Customers are drawn in by Apple's latest technology, whether it's an iPad, iPhone, MacBook, or another of Apple's latest gadgets. People also come to the Apple Store to get help with Apple products they'd purchased.

The CIO's help desk is an internal department, not a retail store. It supports operations around the globe by phone, email, and internet. It also manages the logistics of configuring various computers, parts, and accessories and shipping them to various offices.

Ironically, the department's biggest challenge was employees based in its corporate office, who acted as if the help desk really was an Apple Store. They often bypassed the company's work-order system and walked directly into the IT department to get help. They used their physical proximity to jump to the head of the line and prioritize their needs over projects at remote offices.

For example, a corporate vice president might come in looking for help with her laptop while a help-desk employee was in the midst of getting a network configured for a new office in Europe. It wasn't a comfortable position for the employee. If he dropped everything and helped the vice president, that could put the network project behind schedule. If he asked the vice president to follow the appropriate procedure, that could result in the vice president complaining to the CIO or another executive.

Another challenge was how help-desk employees viewed their role. They didn't think of themselves as perky, customer-focused retail associates like those at the Apple Store. They generally joined the company because they loved computers and wanted to be near cutting-edge technology. They viewed their job as fixing computers and setting up networks rather than helping customers.

The CIO's customer service project had many warning signs that suggested it wouldn't succeed. He was impatient and hoped to find a shortcut. He knew he needed to change the help desk's culture, but he naively thought that could be accomplished through a couple of training classes. He even signaled that the project didn't have his full support by delegating it to one of his managers so he could focus on initiatives he felt were more important.

The biggest challenge of all was that the CIO couldn't describe a successful project outcome. He had a picture in his mind, but it wasn't fully formed.

The best he could do was point to the Apple Store. This didn't sound like a situation where I could be helpful.

I finally asked him, "Have you ever heard of Ron Johnson?" He hadn't.

Ron Johnson and the Tale of Two Companies

Ron Johnson is widely credited for developing the Apple Store and making it successful. Apple hired him in 2000 to be its Senior Vice President of Retail, and he worked closely with CEO Steve Jobs to develop the company's retail concept.

The Apple Store's success is undeniable. In 2011, Johnson's last year there, its $5,626 in sales per square foot was the best mark for any retailer in the U.S.[10] Apple was also named a J.D. Power Customer Service Champion for 2012, recognizing the company's outstanding service from the previous year.

The Apple Store took a fresh approach to retailing in many ways. Its stores were full of products that customers were encouraged to try out. It also had more associates than typical stores, so customers could get hands-on assistance. There were no cashier lines, either; associates rang up purchases using a mobile credit-card reader and an app on their phones.

The centerpiece of each store was the Genius Bar, which was something Johnson invented to help customers get the most out of their Apple products. Johnson described the Genius Bar in a 2011 interview with *Harvard Business Review*: "Imagine a friendly place that dispenses advice and is staffed by the smartest Mac person in town. He would be like a genius to the customer, because he knows so much."[11]

The Genius Bar concept wasn't a hit at first, but Johnson stuck with it. "I had a belief—a conviction—that face-to-face support was going to be much better for customers than phone and web support, which are often really frustrating and ineffective," he explained. "So we stuck with it, and gradually customers started coming."

In November 2011, Johnson was hired away to be the CEO of J.C. Penney. The company was enamored with Johnson's results at the Apple Store, as well as his previous success at Target, where he helped build a strong brand reputation. J.C. Penney's board of directors thought Johnson would be able to work his magic once again and transform a venerable retail brand that had stagnated in recent years.

Johnson felt J.C. Penney's culture was stuck in the past. The company was trying to hang on to tradition instead of evolving to meet its customers' changing needs. Employees had a transaction mindset, where constant sales, coupon programs, and other discounts were used to drive revenue. Perhaps worst of all, Johnson felt the company's leaders were too slow to take action.

Johnson quickly developed an ambitious plan to completely change J.C. Penney's culture.

There were massive layoffs at the corporate office. Johnson brought in a new executive team, many of whom were former Apple colleagues. One of those executives was Michael Kramer, who became J.C. Penney's Chief Operating Officer. Kramer told the *Wall Street Journal*, "I hated the J.C. Penney culture. It was pathetic."[12]

Johnson instituted an autocratic decision-making approach that did away with market research and in-store testing. He announced sweeping changes based solely on his experience and gut instincts. "We didn't test at Apple," said Johnson to one colleague who questioned him.

"Every initiative we pursue will be guided by our core value to treat customers as we would like to be treated—fair and square," said Johnson. He scrapped the company's traditional discounting programs in favor of an everyday low price approach called Fair and Square Pricing. Millions were invested in new store layouts and merchandising agreements with popular brands that he believed would better resonate with J.C. Penney customers.

Johnson also announced plans to create a section in the middle of each store called the Town Square. The Town Square would replace the cosmetic counters and accessories found in the center of a typical department store. Instead, it would feature various services for customers along with monthly attractions like free haircuts during back-to-school season. Johnson said the Town Square concept was similar to the Apple Store's Genius Bar: "Just like in the Apple Store, you have to walk through the products to get to the Town Square."[13]

There was one huge group of employees who were missing from Johnson's bid to overhaul the company culture: store associates. They held tremendous influence over the success of the company's widespread changes because they interacted with customers on a daily basis. An enthusiastic response might help convince lifelong customers that the changes were positive, while a lackluster reception could convince customers to take their business somewhere else.

The associates largely disliked the changes. Many associates felt frustrated that they'd had no input into the company's new direction, and there were widespread accounts of plummeting morale. One store associate told *Business Insider*, "I hate it. I hate the disorder and I hate having my customers give me that look, that 'you don't have any idea what you're doing and I hate this place and I'm never coming back' look."[14]

There was also no change in how associates treated their customers. Customers who walked into a J.C. Penney store just before Johnson became CEO in 2011 were likely to have been ignored. The transactional culture in J.C. Penney stores at the time was largely one of indifference to helping customers on the sales floor. Cashiers believed their job was simply ringing up transactions. Stock associates believed their job was putting stock on the sales floor and arranging displays. After Johnson took over as CEO, company leaders did nothing to change this behavior, and employees still routinely ignored their customers.

Johnson's efforts to transform J.C. Penney ultimately failed. The company's stock sank 40 percent in his first full year. Sales plummeted. J.C. Penney's rating on the American Customer Satisfaction Index fell from 82 when Johnson took over in late 2011 to 77 in 2013.

Johnson was fired in April 2013.

Why Borrowing Another Company's Culture Doesn't Work

The software company CIO and Ron Johnson both failed at their culture initiatives in part because they tried to copy the Apple Store. Their problem was that neither business was comparable to the one they tried to emulate. Each had products, operations, and employees that were different. Each had its own unique history. Even their customers were different.

Johnson built a retail operation from the ground up at Apple. At J.C. Penney, he was trying to change a company that had been in business for over a hundred years. Its employees already had a collective way of thinking, acting, and understanding the world around them. Johnson completely ignored this when he tried to sweep away the J.C. Penney culture and unilaterally impose his own.

Trying to copy another company's culture is an exercise in futility. Every organization is unique. There are too many things that vary from company to company, such as business models, target customers, product line, organizational history, and even the skills and personalities of the individual employees who work there.

That doesn't stop companies from trying to borrow other companies' cultures. Bookstores are stocked with business books that profile service cultures at famous companies, including:

- *The Nordstrom Way*
- *The Disney Way*
- *The Virgin Way*
- *The Cleveland Clinic Way*
- *The Southwest Airlines Way*

Executives from successful, high-profile companies are fixtures on the corporate speaking circuit. Some companies—such as Disney, Zappos, and The Ritz Carlton—have even created business seminars designed to show other companies the inner workings of their unique cultures. These training programs all offer valuable insights and takeaways. Unfortunately, participants mistake the training for a paint-by-numbers blueprint.

People buy the books and attend the trainings hoping to capture the magic that made those famous companies successful. It's easy to forget that the principles and business practices described and discussed weren't developed overnight. Instead, they're a by-product of the unique cultures these companies developed over time. Getting to where they are today took an intense commitment over multiple years.

A book or seminar will not change your culture. It can inspire you. It can give you ideas. But you still have to put in the work to bring your own organization's unique customer-focused culture to life.

Employees often refer to copycat initiatives as a "flavor-of-the-month program." Their company dedicates training and resources to imitate another company, but it never really sticks. The other company is just too different. The other culture doesn't match how this company's employees actually think, act, or understand the world around them. The company's leaders inevitably lose interest and move on to chase after another fad.

In a typical example, a company sent its executives and mid-level managers to a seminar organized by the Disney Institute. The participants were impressed with what they learned, but they compared all the lessons to their own organization's culture. "That sounds cool, but it would never work for us," they thought. By the end of the seminar, the participants had only picked up a few tactics they thought would work.

They returned to their office and set out to implement the few ideas they'd selected. What they didn't understand was that Disney developed its culture by doing *all* of it. These executives were essentially trying to bake a cake with only half the ingredients listed in the recipe. Failure was inevitable.

How Employees Get Lost Without Clear Direction

It's hard for any corporate initiative to succeed if you don't first define a successful outcome. Yet executives like the software company CIO frequently struggle to describe what they want their organization's unique culture to be like. This makes it nearly impossible to get employees aligned around a common way of thinking about, acting upon, and understanding customer service.

In 2013, I did a survey to see how many companies had created a clear definition of outstanding customer service. As you'll learn in Chapter 3, this definition forms the basis of a customer-focused culture because it allows companies to engage their employees in delivering a consistent brand of customer service. Only 62 percent of respondents said their organization had created this definition.

There are several reasons why companies don't define outstanding service for their employees. One reason is that it seems self-evident: people know good and bad service when they see it.

The problem with this thinking is that people tend to have very different definitions of what constitutes great service. On a company level, outstanding service at the Apple Store is vastly different from outstanding service at J.C. Penney. Within a company, different departments have different goals and objectives. Even individual employees have their own ideas and priorities. Failure to align employees' collective thinking typically results in inconsistent customer service.

Some organizations resist creating a customer service vision because they think of it as a lot of marketing fluff. For example, one company created a vision statement that was so long it literally covered the entire wall of their lobby. It was full of impressive-sounding adjectives, but it was also impossible to decipher. Employees snicker at attempts like this that feel inauthentic.

Yet employees need clear direction so they know what's expected of them. Creating a clear definition of outstanding customer service provides this direction, which is critical to creating a customer-focused culture. Chapter 3 gives you step-by-step instructions for developing your customer service vision. Everything else you do should be based on that vision.

That makes Chapter 3 the most important chapter in this book.

What Happens When Culture Becomes a Side Project

Executives are impatient for results. They look for shortcuts and silver-bullet solutions. Furthermore, culture initiatives can easily get relegated to side-project status. Many executives feel these initiatives seem mushy and less easily defined than other activities whose results are simpler to measure.

Here are just a few of the excuses I've heard for delaying a culture initiative:

- "We're knee deep in implementing a new computer system right now."
- "We'd like to work on culture, but we don't have the budget."
- "We're focused on employee engagement this year."

These statements reflect a complete disconnect from what culture really is. Culture should be guiding these initiatives, not taking a back seat. How you approach a system upgrade should be influenced by your culture. It doesn't take a hefty budget to reorient your culture around serving customers. Employee engagement is, by definition, a culture initiative.

One Chief Financial Officer told me his company wasn't ready to focus on culture because they were working on improving customer experience. He told me his executive team didn't see a clear connection between internal culture and customer experience (what a customer thinks and feels about your business). Of course, this link is critical since it's the employees who design and execute the factors that create customer experience.

Some customer service culture initiatives fail because they don't have the appropriate level of executive commitment. A 2015 *Harvard Business Review* report revealed that 51 percent of customer-centricity initiatives are led by someone who isn't a senior executive.[15] The same report found that 64 percent of these projects lack a dedicated team and budget.

One explanation for this is that many companies feel they're already customer-focused. A 2014 study by Execs in the Know and Digital Roots showed that 88 percent of companies felt they were generally meeting the needs and expectations of their customers.

Only 22 percent of customers felt the same way.[16] Another explanation is that companies underestimate the level of time and resources required to build a customer-focused culture. The CEO of one organization delegated a culture initiative to a project team made up of several mid-level managers. It's okay to delegate work, but the CEO completely removed himself from the loop. He assumed the team would keep working on the project without his involvement.

Those project team members had other responsibilities as part of their regular jobs. The CEO focused his communication with these managers on their normal roles and largely ignored the culture project. The initiative quickly took a back seat to day-to-day work, and ultimately stalled out completely. Yet the CEO didn't realize that it was his management that made culture seem unimportant.

Some companies think they can change their culture just by sending frontline employees to training. This rarely works. Training can help employees develop knowledge, skills, or abilities, but while important, these are only a few of the many factors that influence an employee's actual performance. An employee's attitude, influence from their co-workers, and direction from their leaders also play pivotal roles. Likewise, policies, procedures, tools, and resources all impact an employee's ability to serve customers.

I once facilitated a training class for a small organization. It was supposed to be an all-hands meeting, but when I arrived, I learned the organization's leaders had abruptly decided not to attend. Apparently, they felt they had more important things to do.

Two employees approached me after the class. Both were near tears. They told me that they had appreciated the training and learned a lot, but they were concerned that none of it would make a difference. "The people that really needed to be here were our bosses," one of them said. "We really want to serve our customers, but the leaders around here aren't committed to it."

This organization's leaders sent a clear message to their employees that day by skipping out on training that was mandatory for everyone else. They demonstrated that they weren't fully committed. They naively hoped the training would somehow "fix" their employees when it was really their leadership that needed fixing.

Culture isn't a side project. It's a way of doing business that should be integrated into everything you do, and it needs unmistakable executive sponsorship if it's going to work. Building a strong culture takes time and full commitment.

Chapters 5 through 10 are dedicated to providing step-by-step instructions for aligning the most critical aspects of your business with your culture.

Why Culture Initiatives Need a Full Commitment

A client invited me to attend her company's quarterly employee meeting. Employees gathered to hear updates from the CEO and other top executives about financial performance, strategy, key initiatives, and other business issues. The CEO kicked off the meeting by discussing the importance of the company's values.

This wasn't unusual. The CEO talked about the company's values all the time. They represented the company's way of doing business, and the CEO wanted to emphasize their importance. The values described how they wanted to treat their customers, each other, and even their vendors.

Culture wasn't just the CEO's pet project. Every executive at the company regarded culture as a top priority. They used their culture to guide all decisions, whether it was spending money, developing strategy, or training employees. The company's strategy gradually changed over the years as it grew and became even more successful, but the CEO and his top executives never wavered in their full and open commitment to supporting the company's culture. In their minds, it was the culture—above everything else—that made the company successful.

Employees were constantly reminded of the corporate culture. It was embedded in the recruiting process, new hire training, employee development programs, and employees' discussions with their managers. Alignment with corporate culture was assessed during the performance evaluation process. Culture was baked into policies, procedures, and job descriptions.

Culture was deliberately integrated into every aspect of the job.

The company's service obsession paid off. Its customers were consistently delighted, which led to greater loyalty and a lot of word of mouth advertising. At the same time, its employees were highly engaged in delivering the company's unique brand of customer service. Even its vendors embraced the company's service culture and worked hard to provide the company with superior value and service. All these factors combined to help the company achieve a steady growth rate and financial returns well above average.

Their culture emphasized the expectation that they constantly reinforce the culture. They thought culture was important, acted to make it important, and understood it was what helped make them successful.

Other organizations may see some short-term improvement, but find it difficult to sustain a customer-focused culture over the long run.

The wireless communications company Sprint provides an excellent example. The company had never really been known for outstanding customer service, but it sunk to a new low in 2007. That year, it earned a 61 on the American Customer Satisfaction Index (ACSI), which put it well behind its major competitors AT&T, Verizon, and T-Mobile. The company lost over 1,000,000 customers that year, including 1,000 customers whose contracts were infamously terminated for making what the company deemed to be an excessive number of customer service calls.[17]

Dan Hesse was hired as Sprint's CEO in December 2007 to turn the company around. He immediately set about re-focusing the company on customer service. This included establishing a set of core values to guide employee behavior, simplifying pricing plans to make them easier for customers to understand, and making improved customer service a part of every employee's compensation plan. The initial results were promising, with Sprint's ACSI rating climbing from a low point of 56 in 2008 (just a few months into Hesse's tenure) to an industry-leading 72 in 2011.

Remaining at the top proved difficult as other distractions took the focus away from service. In late 2010, Sprint announced a multi-year, $5 billion plan to consolidate its existing network of three different wireless technologies into a single platform.[18] In 2012, SoftBank reached an agreement to acquire Sprint by purchasing 70 percent of its stock. In 2013, Sprint and rival T-Mobile began negotiating a merger that never materialized. By 2014, Sprint's ACSI rating declined down to 68, and its number of retail wireless subscribers decreased 5.6 percent from 2012 to 2014. Hesse left the company by the end of 2014.

A 2013 Towers Watson survey found that only 25 percent of corporate change initiatives succeed.[19] The few companies that do succeed at change initiatives do so through culture. As the Towers Watson report points out, "The best actively build a culture to support and drive behaviors aligned with their business strategy."

Building the right culture is simply too much work for most companies. The few that break through work at it every day. They resist the urge to take shortcuts, and they stick with the initiative for the long-term. These elite few companies understand that culture isn't easy, and they embrace that challenge.

Are you ready for the challenge? Let's go to Chapter 3 where we'll start the process.

Notes:

10 Don Reisinger, "Another Apple Win: Retail Sales Per Square Foot," *CNET*, August 24, 2011. http://www.cnet.com/news/another-apple-win-retail-sales-per-square-foot/.

11 "Retail Isn't Broken. Stores Are," *Harvard Business Review*, December 2011. https://hbr.org/2011/12/retail-isnt-broken-stores-are.

12 Dana Mattioli, "For Penney's Heralded Boss, the Shine Is Off the Apple," *Wall Street Journal*, February 24, 2013.

13 Dana Mattioli, "J.C. Penney Chief Thinks Different," *Wall Street Journal*, January 26, 2012.

14 Kim Bhasin, "Inside J.C. Penney: Widespread Fear, Anxiety, And Distrust Of Ron Johnson And His New Management Team," *Business Insider*, February 22, 2013. http://www.businessinsider.com/inside-jcpenney-2013-2.

15 "Making Customer-Centric Strategies Take Hold." *Harvard Business Review* report, 2015.

16 "Supporting the Connected Consumer in a Multi-Channel Environment: A Comprehensive Survey," *Customer Experience Management Benchmark Series, 2014 Corporate Edition*, Execs In the Know and Digital Roots report, February 2015.

17 Tom Ryan, "Sprint Fires Customers," *Retail Wire*. June, 2007. https://www.retailwire.com/discussion/sprint-fires-customers/.

18 "Sprint Announces Network Vision – A Cutting-Edge Network Evolution Plan With Partners Alcatel-Lucent, Ericsson and Samsung," *Sprint*, December 6, 2010. http://newsroom.sprint.com/news-releases/sprint-announces-network-vision-network-evolution-plan.htm.

19 "Only One-Quarter of Employers Are Sustaining Gains From Change Management Initiatives, Towers Watson Survey Finds," *Towers Watson*, August 29, 2013. https://www.towerswatson.com/en/Press/2013/08/Only-One-Quarter-of-Employers-Are-Sustaining-Gains-From-Change-Management.

Part 2: Building a Customer-Focused Culture

● ● ●

CHAPTER 3

Defining Your Culture

● ● ●

REI's customer service saved Cheryl Strayed's feet.

In *Wild*, her bestselling memoir, she chronicles her 1,100-mile solo hike along the Pacific Crest Trail from California's Mojave Desert to the Oregon and Washington border. Halfway through her journey, Strayed developed constant pain in her feet because her hiking boots were too small. She lost four toenails from them rubbing against the toe boxes of her boots.

Replacing her hiking boots could have been a major problem. Strayed was traveling through a remote part of the wilderness and only encountered civilization every few days. Even then, "civilization" typically meant a campground or small general store where it was unlikely they'd have hiking boots for sale. Her journey took place in 1995, before you could readily order hiking boots, camping equipment, or anything else on the Internet. In any event, she didn't have enough money to replace the pair she was wearing.

Outdoor gear and apparel retailer REI came to the rescue. Strayed had purchased the boots from the retailer, and when a fellow hiker reminded her of its satisfaction guarantee, she called the company to order a replacement pair in a larger size. The customer service representative agreed to ship them to her at no charge.

The timing was incredibly fortuitous. After contacting REI, Strayed still had to hike in her old boots for several days, while her new boots were being shipped to the next post office along the trail. One day, she took off her old boots while resting and accidentally knocked one of them down the mountainside. Since the remaining boot was useless by itself, in a fit of frustration, she threw it down the mountain after the first one. Strayed was forced to walk in camp sandals reinforced with duct tape for the next few days, but she eventually received her new boots.

This wasn't the only way REI's customer service helped Strayed. She'd never been backpacking before starting on her trip, so she relied on knowledgeable associates at an REI store to help her get outfitted with the appropriate equipment. Strayed described her encounters with REI employees in her book: "Every last one of them could talk about gear, and with interest and nuance, for a length of time that was so dumbfounding that I was ultimately bedazzled by it."[20]

In 2014, *Wild* was released as a major motion picture starring Reese Witherspoon. The film stayed true to the story and highlighted REI's role in Strayed's journey without the company having to pay any product placement fees. It was terrific exposure for REI, introducing moviegoers to the outstanding customer service that millions of its customers already knew so well.

It's too simplistic to credit REI's success only to great products and helpful associates. At the heart of all that REI does so well is a customer-focused culture that helps people like Cheryl Strayed enjoy the outdoors.

How REI Provides Employees with a Clear Vision

One piece of equipment Strayed acquired at REI was a compass. She used it to help find her way when the trail wasn't clear.

REI employees have a different sort of compass. The REI mission statement exemplifies a collective way of thinking that points employees in the right direction when taking action to serve customers: *We inspire, educate and outfit for a lifetime of outdoor adventure and stewardship.*

This mission is evident throughout the entire company. Associates are knowledgeable about their products because they're typically inspired to explore the outdoors themselves. In fact, many loyal customers get part-time jobs at REI because they want the employee discount.

REI educates its customers on how to safely tackle new adventures by offering classes on a wide variety of topics such as hiking, climbing, and kayaking.

Policies—such as the 100 percent satisfaction guarantee—are crafted to make it easy for people to get outfitted with the right equipment. The company also invests a great deal of time and money into natural conservation efforts as part of its commitment to environmental stewardship.

REI's mission statement is an example of what I call a customer service vision: a statement that clearly defines the quality of customer service employees are expected to provide. The statement is the foundation upon which a customer-focused culture is formed because it describes a collective way for employees to think about their customers, act to provide outstanding service, and understand how service enables the organization to succeed.

A customer service vision can take many forms. It might be the company's mission statement, like REI, or a customer service guarantee, like Rackspace's Fanatical Support Promise. It might be a corporate vision statement, a set of company values, a customer service slogan, or an internal guide for employees.

What's important is that the customer service vision provides clarity on how to serve customers.

Having a clear customer service vision is a common theme among companies whose employees are obsessed with delivering outstanding customer service. Here are just a few examples from companies with strong customer-focused cultures that you'll learn about later in this book:

- Shake Shack (Chapter 5): *Stand For Something Good*
- Publix (Chapter 7): *Where Shopping Is a Pleasure*
- Safelite AutoGlass (Chapter 9): *Achieve extraordinary results by looking at our business through the eyes of our customers and making it easy for them to do business with us and ensuring their experience is memorable.*

Note that these definitions are all different. Outstanding customer service at a retail store that sells outdoor gear isn't the same as that provided by a fast casual restaurant, a grocery store, or a windshield repair company. There isn't one customer service vision that's right for every organization. You need something unique to your organization.

Perhaps you're not the CEO or owner of a company, but that doesn't mean you can't create a customer-focused culture within your own area of responsibility. Business units, locations, and even individual teams can each create their own customer service vision.

The Center for Sustainable Energy is a nonprofit organization that facilitates clean energy projects for consumers, businesses, and governments. One example is California's Clean Vehicle Rebate Project (CVRP). The State of California provides a rebate for the purchase of zero-emission and plug-in hybrid vehicles. The Center for Sustainable Energy administers the rebate program on behalf of the state.

The customer service team that supports the CVRP has its own customer service vision: *Make it easy to join the clean vehicle movement.* This vision aligns with the organization's overall mission statement: *Accelerating the transition to a sustainable world powered by clean energy.* Having a separate-but-aligned team vision gives the CVRP team specific focus and direction about what they're trying to do for their customers.

Jennifer Rey is the Senior Operations Manager overseeing the CVRP. She uses the department's vision statement to continuously emphasize the importance of customer service with her team. It guides the way employees interact with customers, how the application process is designed, and even the design of the rebate application website. "It has to permeate through everything that you do," Rey explained.

One example of this is a video her team made to educate automotive dealers on the clean vehicle rebate process. Customers often learn details about the rebate program from the salesperson who sold them their vehicle, so it's important for salespeople to provide clear and accurate information. The training video makes it easy for the CVRP team to deliver a consistent message to the large network of dealers selling vehicles that qualify for a rebate.

Culture needs to be clearly defined, whether it's in a large company with thousands of employees or a single team within a small nonprofit. As we discussed in Chapter 2, employees can get lost if they don't have a shared customer service vision or the vision isn't clear.

What Can Happen When There's No Clear Vision

Chances are that your company already has something that could be considered a customer service vision. There might be a mission statement, a list of core values, or a set of service standards. Perhaps your organization has several of these. However, none of them define your company or team culture unless employees can consistently point to one clear message that guides how they serve customers.

One restaurant chain wanted to create a customer-focused culture, but it gave its servers too much to think about. There was a mission statement, an internal service slogan, a set of four service standards, and a 17-step service procedure for serving every guest. All these elements pointed to outstanding customer service, but each sent a slightly different message.

These elements can be called cultural artifacts. A cultural artifact is any statement, symbol, or physical item that helps define an organization's culture. A challenge occurs when an organization has multiple cultural artifacts that don't provide a single direction.

The bevy of cultural artifacts at the restaurant chain created confusion for the servers. Should they focus on the mission, which prioritized creating a great guest experience? Or should they follow their 17-step service procedure, which prioritized consistency and upselling?

I was asked to give a presentation about developing a customer-focused culture at the company's leadership retreat. The senior leadership team and the chain's store managers were all gathered in the room. I displayed a list of all their cultural artifacts and asked, "Which of these is the most important?"

At first, there was silence. Nobody knew the answer because it was something they'd never talked about. Until that moment, these leaders had looked at each cultural artifact individually, but never all together. They suddenly realized why servers were frequently confused about the best way to serve their guests.

The CEO fidgeted uncomfortably in his seat. It's not easy being a leader when your entire team suddenly sees a glaring blind spot in the corporate strategy. But once that blind spot comes to light, it's an important aspect of leadership courage to acknowledge and address the issue head-on.

The CEO turned to the group and asked them to weigh in on which of the cultural artifacts was the priority. As they talked, it became evident that the mission statement resonated most strongly with the leadership team. The group eventually determined that statement should serve as the customer service vision, emphasized over everything else.

This meeting led to some important changes. The restaurant chain pared down its 17-step service procedure to just 10 steps. It aligned the service procedure with the mission statement so the two sent a consistent message. And it integrated the service slogan and service standards into the service procedure itself, so the servers had fewer cultural artifacts to keep in mind.

Many organizations have multiple cultural artifacts that have no real meaning to employees. They have mission statements, vision statements, corporate values, and brand slogans that send conflicting messages or are written in such unclear language that employees don't understand them. Individual departments have their own service slogans and standards, and these don't always align with their corporate counterparts. Employees in these organizations naturally became confused as to what's really most important.

A good customer service vision creates clarity, not confusion. It's okay to have multiple cultural artifacts, but they should all support a single overarching customer service vision that serves as the primary definition of your culture. Employees at all levels of the organization, from the CEO to the front lines, need to have agreement on what their organization's culture stands for.

How to Create a Customer Service Vision

Many companies over-engineer the process of creating their customer service vision. Expensive consultants are hired to spend months conducting research and writing drafts before presenting their recommendations to senior leaders at an executive retreat. The final product is inevitably so convoluted or out of touch with reality that it fails to resonate with employees.

It doesn't have to be that way. A simple, straightforward approach usually works better. There are three steps to creating a customer service vision. The first is gathering input from all stakeholders. The second is writing the vision itself. The third step is validating the vision statement with key stakeholders. Let's take a closer look at each.

STEP 1: GATHER INPUT

Creating a customer service vision shouldn't be an autocratic process driven by a few executives. You want the vision to feel right to employees if it's going to guide their behavior. Therefore, you need to include them in the process.

Here are examples of employee groups you might want to include:

* Frontline Employees
* Middle Management
* Senior Executives

If you're creating a vision for a team or department, you might have a different set to consider:

* Employees on your team
* Your boss
* Key partners in other departments

Customers are the one group you shouldn't consult in this process because this is a future-focused exercise. This may seem counterintuitive, but customers are notoriously bad at telling you what they want. You'll get their input later, when you ask for feedback on how well you're executing the customer service vision.

Once you've identified the stakeholder groups from whom you want input, it's time to gather data. Modern technology makes this easy. You can use an online survey, an internal chat program, or even old-fashioned email.

Even large corporations use this process. In 2003, IBM rewrote its corporate values by holding an online forum that gave every employee the opportunity to contribute their perspective. An estimated 50,000 employees participated from around the world, and the massive discussion generated nearly 10,000 comments. The entire event took place over a span of just 72 hours.[21]

When I help my clients create a customer service vision, I usually gather stakeholder input with an online survey. It's a fast, easy, and inexpensive way to gather data from a large group of people. I use Survey Monkey (www.surveymonkey.com), but there are many other survey programs available.

You can capture everyone's input with just one open-ended question: *What would you like customers to think of when they think about the service we provide?*

The question allows participants to weigh in using their own words. This approach provides a lot of unstructured data in the form of their comments, but it's actually very easy to analyze. I use a text analytics program to create a word cloud, which is a visual depiction of the written comments. The most commonly used words are large and bold, while infrequently used words are less prominent.

Premium Survey Monkey users have access to a word cloud feature, but there are other free word-cloud programs available. One example is Wordle, which allows you to create a word cloud in just a few minutes. You can see some examples and create your own word cloud for free at www.wordle.net.

The word cloud provides a quick visualization of the organization's collective thinking around customer service. For example, when I worked with the Center for Sustainable Energy to create its customer service vision, the three most prominent words in its word cloud were *friendly, like,* and *helpful.* When the group wrote its customer service vision, members of the group discussed these words and why they were important. A consensus quickly emerged: they wanted customers to picture the organization as a friendly person who was so helpful that customers would actually like the process of buying a clean vehicle. That discussion led to what became the organization's final vision statement: *Make it easy to join the clean vehicle movement.* (You can see the team's word cloud here: http://bit.ly/1PpxPSz.)

It's also important to gather examples of existing cultural artifacts relevant to customer service. This may include a company mission statement, vision, values, customer service slogan, or service standards. These will be helpful guides when it comes time to write the customer service vision. If you're writing a customer service vision for an individual team or department, having these cultural artifacts handy will help you align what you create with the organization's overall culture. In some cases, such as the restaurant chain I mentioned earlier, an existing artifact might be chosen to become the customer service vision.

Step 2: Writing the Vision

The next step in creating a customer service vision is to convene a meeting to draft the statement.

You'll accomplish two things in this meeting. The first is the actual writing of the customer service vision; the second is clearly articulating what the vision means through illustrative examples.

I've found through trial and error that the optimal group size for this meeting is seven to 10 people. With more than that, it's too hard to integrate everyone's opinion while you're word-smithing; with fewer, you won't include enough perspectives.

The composition of the group is also important. It should include a representative sample of all levels of the organization, including at least one frontline customer service employee. This will help ensure that multiple perspectives are represented. I've facilitated this exercise many times where a frontline employee has made an important contribution that never would have dawned on a mid-level or senior-level leader.

The meeting should last no more than two hours. This is enough time to write the customer service vision statement while giving people just a little bit of time pressure. Limiting the time causes people to go with their gut and avoid overthinking. This is desirable for writing a customer service vision because we want it to immediately resonate with employees when they read it.

Figure 3.1 is a sample meeting agenda. You can download the agenda from *The Service Culture Handbook* to help write your own vision by visiting www.servicaculturebook.com/tools.

Figure 3.1 Customer Service Vision Writing Agenda

Time: 2 hours

1. **Clarify objectives.**
   - Write a customer service vision statement (share examples)
   - Identify illustrative examples
2. **Review data.**
   - Review survey data (i.e., word cloud)
   - Review existing cultural artifacts (mission, vision, etc.)
3. **Draft vision.**
   1. Split into two teams
   2. Each team drafts a vision statement (15 minutes)
   3. Share drafts and compare
   4. Edit down to one draft
   5. Gut check with the group:
      1. Is the customer service vision simple and easily understood?
      2. Is it focused on customers?
      3. Does it reflect both who we are now and who we aspire to be in the future?
4. **Capture examples.**
   - Identify illustrative stories that exemplify employees living the vision

The first step in the meeting is to clarify the purpose of the meeting: *to write a customer service vision statement and identify illustrative examples that help explain what the vision means.* Be sure to share a few examples of good customer service vision statements from other companies, so participants have an idea of what the end result should look like. (You can find examples from REI, Shake Shack, Publix, and Safelite AutoGlass earlier in this chapter, and more examples throughout the rest of this book.)

The second step is to review the data you've gathered. I typically do this by sharing the word cloud representing all the survey results, plus any existing cultural artifacts pertaining to customer service. We spend just a few minutes as a group discussing our general impressions of the input. (To save time, you may want to share this information with the group prior to the meeting.)

The third step in the meeting is to draft the customer service vision statement. Some organizations already have something that could pass for a customer service vision statement; if you have something like this, start there. As a group, compare the existing statement to the feedback collected to see if it's a match. If so, keep it. If it's close, but not quite there, modify it. If the existing artifact isn't a great match, set it aside and start from scratch. (In my experience, nine times out of ten the group decides to start from scratch.)

Writing even a simple statement is difficult when there are too many opinions involved. To counteract this, divide the group into two teams of three to five people. Give them 15 minutes to draft a vision statement reflecting the input gathered from key stakeholders.

A good customer service vision statement follows these three guidelines:

1. It's simple and easily understood.
2. It's focused on customers.
3. It reflects both who you are now and who you aspire to be in the future.

Let's pause for a moment and look once again at REI's mission statement, which is also its customer service vision. *We inspire, educate and outfit for a lifetime of outdoor adventure and stewardship.* Notice how it fulfills the three criteria: it's simple and direct; it's implicitly customer-focused, even though the word "customer" isn't mentioned; and it's an accurate depiction of who REI is now in addition to being an aspiration for the future.

Okay, let's get back to the writing. Sometimes, groups will finish in less than 15 minutes, but don't let them go longer; time pressure sharpens their thinking. Once both groups have finished, ask them to write their drafts on a piece of flip chart paper or a white board so you can view both simultaneously.

At this point, let the group take a short break: a five-minute pause lets everyone clear their minds, use the restroom if needed, and refill their coffee or water. Ask them not to work on the vision statement while they're taking their break; you want their subconscious brain to take over. Taking a short break allows the participants' strongest thoughts and feelings to percolate to the surface, versus overthinking the process.

When you reconvene, try to reconcile the two team's statements. One way to start is by asking members of one team to describe what they like about the other team's statement. (This is a brainstorming exercise, so don't discuss what's wrong with it!) Then the other team gets to describe what they like about the first team's statement.

Invariably, a few key themes emerge. Sometimes, it's just a key word or two that both groups feel are important. Help the groups combine the best aspects of both drafts until you're able to edit the two drafts down to one clear, simple statement.

Then step back and do a final assessment to see if the statement resonates.

You know you've achieved your goal if the entire group is excited that the customer service vision accurately describes the type of service they'd like to deliver.

You still have work to do if anyone is uncertain. Even a lone voice of dissent can signal that something's not quite right. I've often seen groups discover a weakness in their vision statement because a single person played the role of devil's advocate. If this happens, keep making adjustments until the vision statement clicks with the whole group.

The final step is to develop illustrative examples. These are anecdotes that clearly define behaviors that are aligned with the customer service vision. Later, when you share the vision with the entire organization (or team, department, etc.), the examples will help individuals understand how they can contribute. (We'll cover that part of the process in Chapter 4.)

The examples should be true stories because focusing on what people have already done helps anchor the authenticity of your vision statement. In my experience, if the customer service vision statement is an accurate reflection of the culture, the group never has difficulty coming up with multiple examples.

Step 3: Validating the Vision

The final step in the process is to validate the vision with key stakeholders. This involves sharing that vision with people who weren't part of the writing process to get their reaction.

There are two important reasons for doing this. The first is that the group that wrote the customer service vision statement is susceptible to group think, a phenomenon where group members naturally start thinking alike in a sub-conscious effort to preserve harmony. Validating the customer service vision with a larger group of stakeholders helps ensure that it clearly resonates with people who didn't write it.

The second reason for getting a reaction from key stakeholders is that these are the people who will help achieve buy-in from the rest of the organization. For example, the vision needs enthusiastic support from senior executives since their actions have a significant impact on organizational culture.

Here are a few groups to consider for an organization-wide initiative:

* Senior executives (especially the CEO)
* Junior executives
* Influential departments
* Long-term employees

You may also want to consult union leaders if your employees work under a collective bargaining agreement.

There are multiple ways to engage stakeholders.

* You can accomplish this via one-on-one or small group meetings, especially with busy people like senior executives.
* You can hold focus groups, town hall meetings, or department meetings to share the customer service vision.
* If your group is particularly large, you can use a survey to get input from your stakeholders.

This process is much simpler if you're creating a customer service vision for a single team, department, or business unit. It's easy to share the vision with everyone on the team to get their reaction.

You'll know whether your customer service vision is on target if it receives enthusiastic support. Ideally, you want people to read the statement for the first time and think "Yes! That's us!"

A lukewarm reception generally means there's something that doesn't fully click with employees, which does occasionally happen. If this happens to you, take time to carefully consider the feedback you receive. Think about what adjustments you can make to resolve their concerns. The solution is often as simple as changing one or two words in the statement to get it just right. In rare cases, you may need to reconvene the vision writing team to produce another draft.

Once you've finalized your customer service vision, you're ready to share it with the entire organization (or team, department, etc.). This gives everyone clear and consistent guidance on how your organization wants its customers to be served. It will become the cornerstone of your customer-focused culture.

We'll cover how to do that in Chapter 4.

NOTES:

20 Cheryl Strayed, *Wild: From Lost to Found on the Pacific Crest Trail* (New York: Vintage Books, 2013).

21 Paul Hemp and Thomas Stewart, "Leading Change When Business Is Good," *Harvard Business Review*, December 2004. https://hbr.org/2004/12/leading-change-when-business-is-good.

CHAPTER 4

Engaging Employees with Your Culture

● ● ●

IN 2016, JETBLUE AIRWAYS WAS honored as the top-rated airline for the 12th consecutive year in global market research company J.D. Power's North American Airline rankings. The airline also led all airlines on the American Customer Satisfaction Index (ACSI) for the fourth straight year. This puts JetBlue's customer satisfaction ahead of even the iconic Southwest Airlines.

Leading a competitive industry in customer service for 12 straight years is an astonishing feat. A company has to consistently do a lot right just to lead the pack for one year, let alone for multiple years in a row.

JetBlue regularly does many things that delight its customers. For instance, the airline offers the most legroom in its economy class of any airline.[22] Passengers can access free in-flight television and free internet on most aircraft. JetBlue is also known for its friendly, caring, and helpful employees, whose consistency in serving customers has helped cement its reputation as a customer service leader.

It shouldn't be surprising that JetBlue's CEO, Robin Hayes, credits the company's culture for its success. "JetBlue's distinctive culture is a key competitive advantage. Our 18,000 crewmembers are highly engaged, proud to work for JetBlue and provide outstanding customer service on a daily basis. They truly Inspire Humanity."[23]

JetBlue has numerous initiatives and programs aimed at helping its employees engage with the culture. This tremendous level of engagement is a big part of why JetBlue employees are so obsessed with consistently delivering outstanding service—and why it earned a Top 10 ranking on Forbes's 2016 list of America's Best Employers. "Our people are the heart of the special culture that we cherish," said Hayes. "Our customers feel that—and it's what they love about JetBlue."[24]

How JetBlue Engages Its Employees

An engaged employee is someone who is purposefully contributing to organizational success. This is more elusive than you might think.

Before employees can be engaged with providing outstanding customer service, they must first understand the organization's customer service vision and how they can contribute. A 2013 study by the employee engagement consulting firm BlessingWhite found that the number one employee engagement driver was "greater clarity about what the organization needs me to do—and why."[25]

Employees also need to be committed to actually achieving the company's customer service vision. It's not enough for them to merely complete their assigned tasks; they must buy in to the company culture. Engaged employees regularly look beyond their job description to see how they can make a difference for their customers.

The company's customer service vision consists of its mission statement, *Inspire Humanity*, and its five core values: safety, caring, integrity, passion, and fun. In a time when many airline passengers feel like livestock being herded into an uncomfortable plane by gruff and uncaring employees, JetBlue's customer service vision emphasizes connecting with its customers on a human-to-human level. The airline does much to ensure that its employees, called crewmembers, understand the company's customer service vision and are committed to helping achieve it.

JetBlue is careful to hire people who reflect its culture. In 2015, the company hired only five percent of the more than 140,000 people who applied to work there. Job applicants learn about the JetBlue culture during the screening process, and are selected in part for their compatibility with the customer service vision.

Once they're hired, the airline provides crewmembers with extensive training to ensure that they understand the business and know what's expected. All

JetBlue crewmembers attend a two-day orientation program that introduces new hires to JetBlue's culture and its core business strategies, so they know right up front how they can contribute. Crewmembers also receive specialized training for their individual role (flight attendant, gate agent, etc.), as well as ongoing training that reinforces the importance of the customer service vision and the company's strategic priorities.

The company makes a concerted effort to seek input from crewmembers on managing the business. Executive leaders visit JetBlue locations every quarter to discuss business updates with crewmembers in person, and the company conducts both annual and monthly engagement surveys to solicit crewmember feedback on the quality of their working experience.

JetBlue also has six Values Committees that provide guidance on workplace policies. Each Values Committee represents a different group of employees (airport operations, flight attendants, pilots, etc.), and committees are comprised of crewmembers elected by their peers. The committees influence company policies, work with executive leadership to resolve workplace challenges, and help support company culture.[26]

JetBlue's individual leaders play a pivotal role in keeping crewmembers engaged with the *Inspire Humanity* vision. Laurie Meacham, who leads JetBlue's Social Media, Customer Commitment, and Corporate Recovery Specialist teams, provides a great example. Her teams assist passengers via social media and email, and help resolve passenger complaints that require coordination across multiple departments. She emphasizes the JetBlue culture in nearly everything she does as a leader.

Her teams primarily work remotely out of home offices, but Meacham keeps everyone connected through daily briefings. She also brings her teams together once a quarter for a face-to-face meeting, so people can stay connected on a more personal level while strengthening their commitment to the culture."It's really important to have regular touch points," said Meacham. "If you don't encourage touch points, you risk cultural drift."

Crewmembers also acknowledge each other for outstanding service through a peer-to-peer recognition program. "We like to give shout outs to the team," Meacham explained. Sharing frequent feedback helps crewmembers take responsibility for maintaining the culture amongst their colleagues.

Meacham encourages these interactions between crewmembers because building relationships is a big part of JetBlue's *Inspire Humanity* culture. "It's walking the talk," said Meacham. "We need to do the same thing for our crewmembers that we do for our customers."

This translates to a company that's known for connecting with its customers. For example, some customers are such aviation enthusiasts that they regularly track individual planes in JetBlue's network. When a passenger posted a picture of a particular plane on JetBlue's Facebook page and asked, "Why is this aircraft in San Salvador?" the crewmember who responded knew the details would be important. The crewmember took the time to research the answer, even contacting other departments, before responding. These little details may seem trivial, but they're hugely important to the person who asked the question.

A highly-engaged workforce is a common theme among organizations with customer-focused cultures. Rackspace employees call themselves Rackers because they're passionate about delivering Fanatical Service. REI employees join the company because they're active people who enjoy sharing their enthusiasm for the outdoors with others. Employees at the Center for Sustainable Energy tend to drive fuel efficient cars and carpool to work because they're personally committed to the organization's mission.

Some organizations overlook the importance of employee engagement because many of the people who serve their customers are not company employees. A fast food chain might consist of independently-owned franchises. A start-up consumer products company might outsource its contact center. A furniture store might contract a delivery company to deliver furniture to its customers.

Major League Soccer's Chicago Fire provides an excellent example of how to engage employees who serve your customers, but don't actually work for your company. Their customer service vision is: *To Create the Friendliest, Cleanest & Most Enjoyable Fan Experience in Major League Soccer.* In sports, the outcome of a match has a big impact on the fan's experience, but there are other factors, too. Nicolette Trobaugh, the Fire's Director of Fan Services, says, "We really try to focus on every other aspect of the game to make it the best experience possible."

Most of the people who serve fans at a Chicago Fire match don't actually work for the soccer club. The concessions are run by a contractor who uses a combination of employees and volunteers to serve guests. The stadium itself is owned and managed by the Village of Bridgeview, the town just outside Chicago where the stadium is located. Trobaugh has only a small internal team of employees to help ensure everyone serving guests is delivering a consistent experience.

One factor is making sure staff members are well informed so they can quickly and accurately answer questions and offer assistance. On game days, a member of Trobaugh's team patrols the stadium and quizzes employees on product knowledge, asking questions ranging from the Fire's customer service standards (called Fire Fundamentals) to specific information about that day's match. Employees who correctly answer five out of five questions are given a special chip. Once an employee collects five chips, they can redeem them for Fire merchandise.

The on-the-spot recognition element is key to this program's success. "Nobody likes to be quizzed," says Trobaugh, "but people get competitive when they know they can win a prize." During the 2015 season, more than 50 employees were quizzed at each match with 99 percent of them answering five out of five questions correctly.

Another way the Fire leverages informal communication to improve service is through something called Spark Training. This is a short, pre-shift training session that's focused on helping a specific department (concessions, parking, etc.) address a particular problem. Trobaugh and her team comb through guest survey results to find trends they can address with Spark Training. They use the training to help the vendor "spark" an immediate improvement in that area.

Organizations like JetBlue and the Chicago Fire work hard to develop an engaged workforce. Leaders in these companies understand their success hinges on getting employees to understand and commit to the customer-focused culture.

Numerous studies have linked employee engagement to a better-quality of customer service. For example, Gallup's 2013 State of the American Workplace Report revealed that companies with highly-engaged employees averaged customer satisfaction ratings that were 10 percent higher than companies with a disengaged workforce.[27]

WHAT CAN HAPPEN IF YOU DON'T ENGAGE YOUR EMPLOYEES

A lack of employee engagement causes many problems. Companies struggle to provide consistent service when there isn't a shared customer service vision. Employees are less likely to go the extra mile to serve a customer when they aren't committed to their organization's success. And talented people are more likely to leave a company when they don't feel passionate about the culture.

One organization embarked on an employee engagement initiative designed to get employees to commit to the organization's goal of being the best in its industry. Unfortunately, a series of missteps by senior leaders led to disengaged employees and declining service quality.

One problem was the overall approach. They hired a consulting firm to conduct an employee engagement survey. Cross-functional committees were then formed to study the survey results and recommend improvements to the executive team. This became a bureaucratic process that dragged on for months, with few changes ever being implemented. Even worse, employees weren't surveyed again until 18 months later to see if engagement had improved. By then, many of the employees who had participated in the first survey had left.

Meanwhile, the organization experienced massive budget cuts and layoffs. An initiative designed to help the organization create a customer-focused culture was put on hold and then cancelled due to lack of funding. Employees were now being asked to achieve the same results with fewer resources, and became frustrated and disillusioned with what they saw as unreasonable expectations from senior leaders. Service quality declined as experienced employees left the organization.

Organizations struggle to engage their employees with a customer-focused culture for three reasons.

The first is that a customer service vision has not been clearly delineated, or employees aren't aware of it. Employees can't make a purposeful contribution if the organization hasn't sufficiently defined success and then shared that definition.

The second reason is that employees' commitment hasn't been secured. Amazingly, many organizations aren't even trying to engage their employees. A 2015 study from the consulting firm Deloitte found that just 28 percent of respondents agree that their organization had an up-to-date employee engagement strategy.[28]

The third reason companies struggle with employee engagement is that senior leaders themselves aren't fully committed. Some companies just focus on engaging new employees, which can result in the more tenured employees becoming disengaged. A 2015 study by the employee engagement software provider Quantum Workplace found that employees who have been on the job for three to five years are 17 percent less engaged than employees who are still in their first year with the company.[29]

Deloitte's 2015 survey revealed that engaging employees with the corporate culture was the most important human resources challenge faced by organizations around the world. The same study found that less than half of the participants felt their companies were ready to address the issue.

Many companies treat their employee engagement efforts like a side project rather than an essential part of their business. A typical organization approaches engagement by administering an organizational climate survey to employees every 12 to 18 months. These surveys look at core drivers of job satisfaction, but often don't assess the two essential elements of engagement:

1. Does the employee understand the customer service vision?
2. Is the employee committed to helping achieve it?

Conducting a survey only every 12 to 18 months makes it difficult to enact meaningful changes or assess the effectiveness of whatever improvements are attempted. Most companies following this model appoint a committee to study the results and make recommendations to the executive team. It typically becomes a long, drawn-out bureaucratic process where few changes or improvements are actually implemented.

Engaging employees isn't for the faint of heart. It requires a lot of work and commitment that many leaders aren't prepared for. But if you're up for it, you can use the following step-by-step plan to get there.

How to Engage Your Employees
There are three major steps to getting your employees to commit to a customer-focused culture:

1. The initial roll-out of your customer service vision.
2. Reinforcing your vision.
3. Assessing employee engagement levels.

Each of these steps is essential to engaging employees, whether your focus is on the entire workforce or an individual team within an organization.

Step 1: Rolling Out Your Customer Service Vision
This step begins with the assumption that you've already created a customer service vision that clearly defines the level of service your employees are expected to provide. You can't engage your employees without this unambiguous statement of purpose, so it's an important starting point. (You'll find a step-by-step guide for creating a customer service vision in Chapter 3.)

With your vision in place, the first step to getting your employees to commit to it is to develop a communication plan for introducing it to the entire organization (or individual team, department, or location if that's the scope of your initiative). Start by creating a goal for developing this plan, and then work backwards to determine how you can accomplish it.

Your communication goal should be to ensure that all employees can answer three specific questions about the customer service vision:

1. What is it?
2. What does it mean?
3. How do I personally contribute?

You should, of course, know the answers to these questions yourself before designing your communication plan. If you haven't done this already, now is a good time to create an answer key. The answer key should outline the types of answers you'd expect to see, rather than required verbatim responses. It's actually best if employees answer these questions in their own words; this isn't an exercise in memorization. What's important is that employees understand the customer service vision and know how to use it to guide their performance.

Creating an answer key for the third question can be tricky because employees in different roles, departments, or locations generally make different contributions to customer service. For example, imagine a restaurant that strives to provide a comfortable, family-friendly experience for guests. The hosts might say they contribute by making families feel welcome. The servers might say they ensure families have an enjoyable experience during their meal. Bussers might say they keep tables clean and glasses filled so families remain comfortable. The cooks might say they prepare delicious meals so families enjoy dining out without having to wait too long. All of these answers tie back to an overarching theme, but in each instance, they're also tied to the employee's specific role.

Once you've created your answer key, identify a communication plan to ensure employees know the answers. There's no single best way to communicate your customer service vision. Your specific plan will depend on how many employees you need to reach, where they're located, and what communication systems your company already has in place. There are many ways to do this, but here are a few examples:

- Have the CEO announce the customer service vision in a company-wide communication.

- Leverage existing communication vehicles, such as internal chat programs, email, employee newsletters, bulletin boards, and intranet sites.

- Produce a short video that explains the customer service vision. (You can see a great example from Rackspace here: https://youtu.be/WhhpzZWXBk8)

- Create signs, posters, and job aids to distribute to various parts of the company.

- Develop a short training program to introduce the customer service vision to employees.

- Conduct a train-the-trainer session for organizational leaders, so they'll know how to introduce the customer service vision to their teams in a consistent way.

- Ask team leaders to meet with their employees as a team or one-on-one to discuss the customer service vision.

A good communication plan includes both variety and repetition.

You want to communicate through a variety of methods so you capture your audience's attention and they don't tune you out. And you should repeat the same message through each of those communication methods because repetition is the key to anchoring new ideas into long-term memory.

You can download a communication plan worksheet at www.serviceculturebook.com/tools. Figure 4.1 is a sample communication plan from a mid-sized software company I worked with.

Figure 4.1: Customer Service Vision Communication Plan

Phase One: Announcement
A. Share the customer service vision via company-wide communication from the CEO
B. Reinforce the vision via messaging from the corporate communications department
C. Display the vision on signage and posters at all company locations

Phase Two: Initial Training

D. Hold town hall-style kick-off meetings at each location to discuss the vision

E. Create one-page job aids to distribute to all employees

F. Provide employees with mugs, t-shirts, and other items to support the vision

Phase Three: In-Depth Training

G. Integrate the customer service vision into existing customer service training programs

H. Have managers follow up with employees after the training to observe them using the vision to guide their daily work

I. Integrate the vision into an existing employee feedback form used by managers to coach employees on their performance

The communication plan helped ensure all the software company's employees understood the customer service vision and how they contributed. This translated to higher engagement levels, where employees understood what made the company successful and took the initiative to solve pressing customer service challenges on their own without prompting from their managers.

STEP 2: REINFORCING THE CULTURE

Many customer-focus initiatives fail when there's a big rollout with a lot of fanfare but no plan to sustain it. Slowly but surely the initiative fades from employees' memories as they're consumed with daily tasks and work assignments.

The way to avoid this problem is by continuously reinforcing the culture with employees long after the initial rollout, consistently reminding them of the customer service vision and fostering employee commitment.

Just like the rollout communication plan, there's no one-size-fits-all solution. The size of your organization, your existing culture, and whether you're engaging an entire company or an individual team all have an impact on how you approach ongoing reinforcement. What matters is that you create reinforcement programs that are right for your situation.

For example, let's recap some of the ways JetBlue reinforces its customer-focused culture with crewmembers:

- Reinforcement messages from the CEO in corporate communications.
- Quarterly in-person business updates from executive leaders.
- Values Committees that support and reinforce the culture.
- A peer-to-peer program where crewmembers recognize their co-workers.
- Leaders like Laurie Meacham who model the culture on a daily basis.

Companies with highly-engaged employees often use the performance evaluation process to reinforce the culture. Employees receive feedback on behaviors that align with the culture, as well as suggestions for improvement. In some organizations, the performance review process helps ensure employees are championing the culture before they can be considered for a promotion.

No matter how much coaching, training, or feedback they get, there are still some employees who can't or won't fit in. Keeping these employees in the organization can be toxic, since it sends an implicit signal to others that these employees' actions are acceptable. Also, sometimes employees who don't fit in actively attempt to persuade other employees to undermine the culture, as well. In this case, it's imperative to act quickly to terminate these employees.

This is a true test for many organizations. Some customer service leaders are willing to overlook an employee who doesn't fit with the culture, as long as they're productive. Other leaders just don't have the heart to let someone go, even if their presence is hurting the performance of other employees or causing good employees to leave the organization. But companies with highly-engaged employees actively work to remove employees who can't or won't fit with their culture.

Letting an employee go doesn't have to be heartless. One of my favorite examples involved a manager named Mike. He was a productive employee who just couldn't fit in with his company's culture. His boss finally reached a point where it was time to cut Mike loose.

The Human Resources Director at the company knew Mike had the potential to be a good employee, so he called a colleague at another company in town where he thought Mike would be a better fit. The HR Director arranged for Mike to have an interview at the other company later that day. When Mike was called in to meet with his boss and the HR Director, he was informed that he was being let go, but he was also told about the interview. Mike ended up getting the job at the new company, where he became a terrific employee who was a good fit with that company's culture.

STEP 3: ASSESSING EMPLOYEE ENGAGEMENT

It's critical that you periodically assess employee engagement. The purpose of the assessment should be to evaluate existing levels of employee engagement and identify opportunities to make things even better. The stronger your employees' understanding of the customer service vision, and the stronger their commitment to helping achieve it, the stronger your culture will be.

Many people instantly think of an annual employee engagement survey, but there are other options to consider. One alternative is to use the performance review process to assess engagement, since engagement and performance are both measures of contributions to organizational success. This helps you identify individuals and teams whose contributions to the culture are flagging, and initiate honest dialogue with these people to understand the reasons why.

One of my clients provided its managers with leadership training to help them become more comfortable with having these performance discussions on a regular basis. Individual contributors were also trained in a parallel program, so they could do a better job of handling their end of the feedback discussion with their manager. My client then hired me to facilitate meetings with each of its locations and departments to help managers and their employees establish team norms for engaging in an ongoing performance dialogue. As you might have guessed, these discussions were all centered on reinforcing the company's culture.

Another option is to rely on direct, informal dialogues with employees. This approach works particularly well in smaller organizations or on individual teams. For example, you might have regular conversations with employees to assess whether or not they have clarity on those three essential questions:

1. What is the customer service vision?
2. What does the customer service vision mean?
3. How do I personally contribute to the customer service vision?

Nicolette Trobaugh and her Fan Experience team at the Chicago Fire used a version of this approach with their match day quizzes. Coming up with a fun way to spot check employees' knowledge of their customer service expectations helped generate enthusiasm for the fan-focused culture.

Here are a few suggestions if you decide to conduct an employee engagement survey. First and foremost, I suggest measuring employee engagement more than once per year. Imagine measuring anything else that's important to the business just once a year! How could you manage your budget if you only looked at your finances annually? Similarly, how can you improve customer service if you only ask for feedback on customer service levels once every twelve months?

The problem is that a survey is just a snapshot in time. Employee engagement survey results are primarily impacted by an employee's most recent experiences. That means a positive or negative experience shortly before the survey is launched has a disproportionate effect on the results. There's even a joke among some managers that the best way to boost your employee engagement scores is to throw a pizza party for your team right before the annual survey goes out. A few managers I know have actually held off on disciplinary action with employees until after the engagement survey to avoid getting a low score from a potentially disgruntled team member.

The other problem with only doing an annual survey is that if you implement any changes as a result of the feedback, you won't know if they're effective until a year later. That's too long to make the survey a meaningful measurement, since so many other changes will happen during that time.

The economy could rise or fall, the company could launch a new product or close down a division, or a wave of new employees could join the company. Variables such as these make it difficult to compare survey results from year to year.

An alternative for larger companies is to divide your employee base into 12 random groups and survey one group every month. This provides a monthly snapshot of employee engagement while surveying each employee only once per year. Or you can survey all employees once per year, but conduct short check-in surveys with sample groups of employees once per month.

However you choose to do it, getting engagement data more frequently than once a year will help you be more responsive to workplace climate issues, since you'll be able to compare your progress from month to month.

This may seem like a lot of work, but we're actually just getting started. Engaged employees will only stay engaged if they perceive their company truly believes in the customer service vision. They want to see the organization and its leaders walk the talk. That's difficult to do on a consistent basis, but we'll lay out a plan for making it happen in Part 3.

NOTES:

22 Most legroom in coach claim," *JetBlue*, December 21, 2016. http://www.jetblue.com/travel/planes/.

23 JetBlue, "Hayes's letter to shareholders" (excerpt), *JetBlue 2015 Annual Report*.

24 "JetBlue Named Top 10 Place to Work in Forbes' 'America's Best Employers of 2016' List," *JetBlue*, March 23, 2016. http://www.businesswire.com/news/home/20160323006015/en/JetBlue-Named-Top-10-Place-Work-Forbes'.

25 BlessingWhite, *Employee Engagement Research Report 2013*, 2013.

26 JetBlue, *Business, Social, and Environmental Sustainability*, 2015. https://www.jetblue.com/p/JetBlueResponsibilityReport2015.pdf.

27 Gallup, Inc., *2013 State of The American Workplace*, 2013. http://employeeengagement.com/wp-content/uploads/2013/06/Gallup-2013-State-of-the-American-Workplace-Report.pdf.

28 Dan Brown, Sonny Chheng, Veronica Melian, Kathy Parker, and Marc Solow, "Global Human Capital Trends 2015," *Deloitte University Press,* February 2015.

29 Quantum Workplace, *2015 Employee Engagement Trends Report*, 2015.

Part 3: Changing Your Company's Service DNA

● ● ●

CHAPTER 5

Aligning Your Business Around a Customer-Focused Culture

● ● ●

SHAKE SHACK IS A NEW York City institution. It originated in 2001 as a temporary hot dog cart in Madison Square Park to help fund the park's revitalization. The cart became an instant hit, drawing huge crowds and long lines when the weather was nice.

In 2004, the city decided to replace the hot dog cart and install a permanent food kiosk in the park. Restaurateur Danny Meyers's Union Square Hospitality Group had been running the hot dog cart even though his company was best known for its fine dining restaurants, including the Union Square Café and Gramercy Tavern. The company decided to bring its fine dining expertise to a reimagined version of a roadside burger stand, which led to the opening of the first Shake Shack, a fast casual restaurant selling burgers, hot dogs, fries, and frozen custard.

Today, Shake Shack's popularity is stunning. At this writing, there are eight locations in New York City alone, and a total of 19 in New York State. The lines are so famously long at its original Madison Square Park location that the company installed a Shack Cam so people could go online and judge the size of the crowd before deciding whether to head over. In 2015, the *Wall Street Journal* published an article outlining the optimal times to get in the Shake Shack line at Citi Field when attending a New York Mets baseball game. Many tourists who come to New York include Shake Shack on their "must visit" list.

The chain's popularity is also growing outside New York City. By 2016, Shake Shack had locations in 14 states, the District of Columbia, and a growing list of international restaurants in cities such as London, Istanbul, Dubai, Moscow, and Tokyo.

The company has won a string of accolades as it's grown. It was named one of the 25 Most Innovative Consumer and Retail Brands in 2014 by Entrepreneur.com. And in 2015, Shake Shack won the Wisetail Award, which recognizes innovators in Learning and Development, for its employee engagement.

People flock to Shake Shack because of its outstanding food and for the experience. Employees are friendly, outgoing, and well trained. Despite the huge crowds, they're attentive to their customers and keep their restaurants clean. In some strange way, many people feel that waiting in line at Shack Shake along with all the other enthusiastic customers is part of the fun.

The company went public in 2015. Its first annual report highlighted the customer-focused culture as its top competitive strength: "We believe that the culture of our team is the single most important factor in our success."[30]

How Shake Shack Aligns Everything Around Culture

Shake Shack's customer service vision is *Stand For Something Good*. This vision stretches beyond the high level of customer service it tries to deliver: it's a strategic guide for managing the entire company.

Shake Shack aligns key operational decisions around its customer service vision, ensuring that everything it does reinforces the culture. You can see this alignment in five key areas:

1. Goals
2. Hiring
3. Training
4. Empowerment
5. Leadership

Let's take a closer look at each of them.

Goals

The company has a goal of adding 10 new domestic company-operated Shake Shacks per year. Given its popularity, it could easily grow at a much faster rate. However, the operation has limited its growth rate to ensure it can maintain focus on its *Stand For Something Good* culture. It's concerned that growing too rapidly could compromise the supply chain, food quality, hiring, training, site selection, or other factors that give the chain its unique identity.

Every Shake Shack employee is given a stake in the company's success through a revenue-sharing program paying one percent of top line revenue on a monthly basis. The program, called *Shack Bucks*, adds two dollars per hour to the average employee's paycheck.[31] The Shack Bucks program helps every employee stay focused on the company's overall success.

Hiring

Shake Shack hires employees who embrace its customer service vision. The company looks for what they call "51%'ers": people who are warm, friendly, motivated, caring, self-aware, and intellectually curious.[32] The idea is to hire for fit with the company's culture and then train employees on the technical skills required to do their jobs. This hiring practice helps reinforce the culture because new employees are already known to be a good fit.

The company has a web page that offers extensive information about its culture, core values, and what it's like to work at Shake Shack. This makes it easy for prospective hires to understand exactly what type of person the company is looking for.

Training

Shake Shack employees receive extensive training, and the first priority for every new hire is to learn about the company's culture. Employees are taught how to incorporate the company's five core values into their daily work. Of course, they also receive training on customer service, the Shake Shack menu, their individual jobs, and food safety.

Shake Shack has a promote-from-within philosophy focused on developing employees into future leaders who can help others follow its customer service vision. The company cross-trains employees to help them learn a variety of skills, and publishes a career ladder showing how they can advance to higher positions within the company. Leadership training is also available to help employees develop the skills necessary to move into management positions.

Empowerment

Employees are empowered to go beyond their normal routine to delight their customers. The company's CEO, Randy Garutti, described the company's empowerment philosophy to a group of new employees before a store opening: "Put us out of business because you are so damn generous with what you give the people who walk in this door. If there's a kid crying, who's going to walk over with a free cup of custard? I challenge you to put us out of business with how generous you are. Go do it. Give away free stuff."[33]

Empowerment involves more than just giving employees the authority to go above and beyond to serve customers. It also includes processes carefully designed to make it easy for Shake Shack's employees consistently fulfill the vision. Employees receive detailed instructions on best practices for completing daily tasks, such as food preparation, maintaining restaurant cleanliness, and serving guests. These processes prioritize quality over speed. For example, Shake Shack's burgers are cooked following a highly detailed procedure that takes far more time and effort than a typical fast casual restaurant. It's designed to create the unique flavor that customers love.

Leadership

Finally, Shake Shack's leaders are fully committed to its vision. Senior management uses *Stand For Something Good* to guide all their decisions. The company provides extensive leadership training so its store-level leaders know how to use the vision as their guide. Garutti visits multiple locations every week to reinforce the company's vision with store managers and employees. Managers meet with their employees daily to review goals and discuss opportunities for continued improvement.

Aligning all of these actions around Shake Shack's *Stand For Something Good* vision enables the company to consistently reinforce the culture. The company even works with external stakeholders, such as suppliers, to help them understand the customer service vision so they can operate under the same guidelines when doing business with Shake Shack. This alignment is the secret to its ability to consistently impress its customers in a way that bedevils most other companies.

The other customer-service-obsessed companies profiled in this book follow a similar blueprint. Rackspace hires people who can embrace giving *Fanatical Support* and then empowers those employees to consistently go above and beyond. Bright House Networks, a cable company you'll meet in Chapter 9, designed a new process to make it easier for customer service reps to make judgment calls on giving account credit, and then tasked its managers with coaching reps to ensure those judgment calls consistently align with the vision. Zendesk, a software company you'll meet in Chapter 12, created a customer service vision, and then its senior leaders aligned the organization's management philosophy around those values.

Culture at these companies is constantly reinforced by aligning multiple operational facets around the specific customer service vision. This process is so rigorous in customer-focused companies that it becomes embedded in the organizational DNA, making service a fundamental part of how employees at these companies think, act, and understand the world around them.

WHAT CAN HAPPEN IF YOUR BUSINESS AND CULTURE AREN'T ALIGNED

Alignment can support and reinforce an organization's culture, but a lack of alignment can undermine any culture-building efforts. It's not enough to develop a clear customer service vision and communicate that vision to employees. The vision only becomes real if it matches what people are actually doing. This means it must be constantly reinforced within employees' daily work.

Let's look back at the Comcast account cancellation example from Chapter 1 to see how misalignment contributed to that company's dismal customer service reputation. If you recall, a Comcast customer named Ryan Block had such a difficult time trying to cancel his account that he started recording the call halfway through. Block posted the recording online and it quickly went viral.

We can start by assuming that Comcast doesn't actually provide poor customer service on purpose. After all, its public apology to Block described this situation as an unusual occurrence:

> "While the overwhelming majority of our employees work very hard to do the right thing every day, we are using this very unfortunate experience to reinforce how important it is to always treat our customers with the utmost respect."

However, Comcast's core business processes in the summer of 2014 were misaligned with this notion of always treating customers with the utmost respect. You can see this in a strategy that prioritizes short-term revenue over long-term customer satisfaction. That's why the company hired Retention Specialists whose goal is to keep customers from canceling. These Retention Specialists have goals and incentives for preventing cancellations, not for keeping customers happy. They receive extensive training on overcoming objections and preventing cancellations, not for how they can make the cancellation process as easy as possible.

The account cancellation process itself was intentionally designed to make canceling an account difficult. Customers are required to call, even though they can handle many other transactions through the company's online self-service function. When a customer got a Retention Specialist on the phone, that employee wasn't empowered to deviate from a process carefully designed to block cancellation attempts. Respect for the customer's time was outweighed by the company's goal to secure short-term revenue.

Finally, Comcast's leaders reinforced the notion that capturing short-term revenue was more important than customer satisfaction. They evaluated employees based upon their retention statistics, not their service quality. Bonus programs were implemented to reward employees for talking customers out of canceling, and employees could actually lose money if they weren't successful.

All those things pointed employees toward stonewalling customers who tried to cancel. An employee who politely canceled a customer's account without hesitation would have been violating Comcast policy.

Clearly, the company's operations were misaligned with the notion of providing outstanding service.

Comcast is an easy target for this discussion because so many parts of its operation have been directly opposed to serving customers. Other companies may have a few business practices pointed towards a customer-focused culture, but employees still receive confusing messages because the organization isn't fully aligned.

One example happens when managers set a target score for a customer satisfaction survey, and then become fixated on achieving the goal without regard for how it's achieved. They implement incentives to encourage employees to achieve high scores or threaten to punish employees with write-ups or termination if their scores fall below a certain level. This has the effect of encouraging employees to manipulate customers into giving them a good survey score rather than using the survey for its intended purpose of gathering constructive customer feedback.

Getting too focused on achieving a goal without understanding its connection to the customer service vision is just one of the potential problems caused by misalignment. Companies routinely hire employees who are a poor fit for their culture because leaders are anxious to fill positions at a low cost. New employees in many companies are given little to no customer service training, so they can't possibly know how to fit in with the company culture or live up to the customer service vision. Processes are frequently designed to control and standardize behavior rather than empowering employees to delight their customers. And leaders in many companies spend shockingly little time coaching and training their teams to reinforce the customer service culture.

Another misalignment occurs when different departments within an organization fail to embrace the same customer service vision. This inevitably causes inconsistent service and harms the company's reputation.

Customer service channel management provides an excellent example. A customer service channel refers to the method a customer uses to contact a company for customer service. Customers typically have multiple channel options when contacting a company, such as the phone, email, a self-service website, or one of several social media platforms like Twitter or Facebook. A customer might also be able to visit one of the company's physical locations to try to resolve the problem in person.

In many companies, misalignment occurs because these various channels are managed by different departments. Phone and email could be operated by a contact center, the website might be run by the marketing department, and social media by the company's communications department. The physical locations could be managed by another department known as retail operations. If these departments approach customer service differently, they create an uneven experience for the customer—and that hurts the company's brand.

One side effect happens when companies inadvertently encourage customers to air their grievances on Twitter. A 2016 study by Execs in the Know, a customer experience networking organization, found that social media was solely managed by the Marketing or PR function in 46 percent of companies, with no involvement by the customer service department. The managers in these departments are often more empowered to resolve issues than their counterparts answering phone calls, emails, or other contacts.[34]

This means that angry customers who vent their frustration on Twitter about a go-nowhere customer service call often get a fast response and a swift resolution. Many customer service leaders tell me social media complaints get higher priority than complaints submitted via other channels. Since these complaints are public, corporate executives worry about a negative image. As a result, customers soon realize that they can complain via Twitter any time they need assistance.

This kind of misalignment can create mistrust among employees. People in one department might blame another team for poor service, and vice versa. These issues rarely get fixed, and instead are allowed to continue. A 2016 study by my consulting firm, Toister Performance Solutions, revealed that 36 percent of contact center employees facing a severe risk of burnout at work felt their coworkers did not deliver outstanding customer service.[35]

You can see from these examples that alignment is at fault when a company espouses a certain brand of customer service while employees act in a completely different way.

How to Check Your Customer Service Alignment

Chapters 6 through 10 detail how to align the five operational cornerstones of a customer-focused culture: goals, hiring, training, empowerment, and leadership. Each chapter focuses on a specific concept and provides step-by-step guidance for aligning that concept with your customer service vision.

For now, a good starting point is to check your organization's overall alignment using a short assessment. It's a quick way to determine areas of strength and identify opportunities for improvement. I've listed the five assessment questions below, or you can download a copy at www.serviceculturebook.com/tools. (You can also use this tool to assess the alignment of an individual team within your organization.)

Having a customer service vision is a prerequisite for completing this. You can't gauge your company's cultural alignment unless you have something with which you're trying to align. If you haven't done this yet, I suggest revisiting Chapter 3 for step-by-step instructions on creating your vision.

Start by rating your organization on the five statements contained in the assessment. Use a scale of 1 (Almost Never) to 5 (Almost Always). Be brutally honest about your scores, since an artificially high score will only hide opportunities for improvement.

1. We set business goals that represent progress toward our customer service vision.
2. We hire employees who are passionate about our customer service vision.
3. Employees are given sufficient training to teach them how to deliver service that fits our customer service vision.

4. Employees are empowered with the authority, resources, and work procedures they need to fulfill our customer service vision.
5. Organizational leaders reinforce our customer service vision with their employees on a daily basis.

Tally up your scores to get your total. This gives you a summary alignment score for your organization or team. Compare your total score to the alignment key below.

Alignment Key:

- **A score of 20 to 25 indicates alignment**. Your organization is well positioned to deliver outstanding customer service.
- **A score of 15 to 19 indicates partial alignment.** Many aspects of the organization are aligned with your culture, but there are some areas for improvement.
- **A score of 14 or less indicates misalignment.** Your organization's lack of alignment may be causing poor customer service. There are significant areas for improvement.

Looking at your overall score as well as the individual ratings for each category, try to identify areas where you feel your organization or team is aligned—and also look for specific areas where there can be improvement.

The categories are there to be helpful, but don't get too hung up on where your organization falls. This assessment is meant to be more of a conversation starter than a definitive analysis of your organization's alignment.

It's interesting to complete this assessment for multiple departments to see how they compare. Start by assessing your organization as a whole. Next, complete the same assessment for individual departments that have direct or indirect customer contact. Compare the results to see if some teams are more aligned than others.

Now you're ready to read the following chapters, which give you step-by-step instructions for each of the five cornerstones of a customer-focused culture.

NOTES:

30 Shake Shack, *2014 Annual Report*

31 Rob Brunner, "Shake Shack leads the better burger revolution," *Fast Company*, June 2015. http://www.fastcompany.com/3046753/shake-shack-leads-the-better-burger-revolution.

32 Shake Shack, *2014 Annual Report*.

33 Rob Brunner, "Shake Shack leads the better burger revolution," *Fast Company*, June 2015. http://www.fastcompany.com/3046753/shake-shack-leads-the-better-burger-revolution.

34 Execs In The Know, *The Corporate Perspective: Exploring Multi-Channel Customer Care*, Customer Experience Management Benchmark Series, February 2016.

35 Jeff Toister, "How to Battle Agent Burnout." *Toister Performance Solutions* white paper, 2016: www.toistersolutions.com/burnout.

CHAPTER 6

Setting Goals That Drive Your Culture

● ● ●

SHOPPING FOR A CAR CAN be a daunting task. There is an overwhelming number of makes and models to choose from, and it's hard to know if you're getting a good deal. That's why many car buyers use an independent review site like Cars.com.

Cars.com helps consumers research new and used vehicles and find the make and model that best fits their needs. They can use the site to get pricing information and check to see if dealers in their area have the car or truck they want in stock. Customers also use the website to search for reputable mechanics.

Cars.com has built a reputation for outstanding customer service. In 2015, it was ranked as the top automotive review site for the third straight year.[36] The company has an industry-leading 85 percent customer satisfaction rating for its phone support. And its contact center won the International Customer Management Institute's 2014 award for best customer care team in the small- to medium-sized contact center category.

Like other organizations profiled in this book, employees at Cars.com are obsessed with serving their customers. Cars.com's parent company, TEGNA, Inc., defines its customer service vision this way: *Empowering the people we serve to act with conviction and navigate their world successfully.* That's exactly what its employees try to do for people who are purchasing a new vehicle. They try to take a complicated and important purchasing decision and give people the information and tools they need to act with confidence.

There's one aspect of building a customer-focused culture where Cars.com particularly excels: getting employees to buy into its culture by using goals and metrics to drive behavior.

HOW CARS.COM USES GOALS TO DRIVE ITS CULTURE

Cars.com measures customer satisfaction, or CSAT, via customer surveys. Like many companies, Cars.com's leaders set CSAT goals in an effort to motivate employees to go the extra mile to help improve service quality. What makes Cars.com different from most organizations is how they connect CSAT goals and other metrics to their customer service vision.

Heather Rattin, the company's Vice President of Operations, runs the customer care team. She and her team use their survey data to continuously refine the customer experience and make it easier for car buyers to use their site. Rattin is careful to avoid fixating on a target CSAT score. Instead, her goal is to make it as easy as possible for consumers to use the company's site, so Cars.com becomes their preferred source for car-buying information.

CSAT survey data alone doesn't always provide all the answers. Rattin and her team create a story by combining this data with other information, such as the volume of customer service inquiries, the specific reasons people contact customer care, and comments on individual surveys. "We use this data to catch trends with individual employees, but also with our products," she explains. For instance, her team was able to use customer comments from surveys with low scores to identify and fix a user interface issue on its website that hadn't been discovered in testing.

Rattin also looks to her employees to help improve the product and customer support processes by sharing their feedback. For instance, "We look at what confuses new hires in training, because they're coming at it from a fresh perspective," Rattin says. At the end of each week of training, the trainer conducts a roundtable discussion with new hires to discuss things they think could be improved. Their suggestions and ideas are then shared with the company's training team and senior management for consideration.

The customer care team at Cars.com also uses an internal communication platform, called Chatter, to share ideas for improving service. Employees are asked to answer two questions when contributing their ideas. First, why is this better for the customer? And second, why is it better for the customer care agent? Rattin believes that understanding why things are done a certain way helps employees become more committed to a process, even if it requires a little extra effort. It's easier for them to suggest actionable ideas for improvement because they understand how a process or procedure fits into the big picture.

The company has also encouraged employee feedback by helping its managers get better at listening. According to Rattin, "A lot of our focus has been on training managers and team leads to listen carefully to their employees and get to the heart of issues."

As an example, managers discuss customer service survey data with their employees on a daily basis. Rattin believes this dialogue between managers and their employees is necessary so they can work together to investigate why metrics like CSAT are trending in a certain way. The collaboration helps employees feel invested in finding ways to improve service and then take pride in knowing they helped create the solutions.

Combining CSAT data with other metrics has also helped Rattin make a business case for investing more in the company's customer care team. When the team needed an upgraded knowledge management system, Rattin combined CSAT data with productivity figures to pitch the investment to the company's CFO. A knowledge management system is a database of company information that makes it easier for employees and customers to answer questions, and Rattin was able to show how a new system would make customers happier and also save Cars.com money, since employees would use the upgraded tool to serve customers faster.

The way Cars.com approaches customer service goals echoes a common theme at many companies with customer-focused cultures. Like many organizations, these companies typically have goals for key metrics like CSAT, customer loyalty, and cost savings. However, customer-focused companies are careful not to get too focused on meeting any one metric without considering the overall impact. Leaders at these companies combine data from multiple sources, share this information with employees, and involve employees in finding ways to continuously improve. The ultimate goal is to drive behavior that's aligned with their customer service vision.

Fidelity's Workplace Solutions division provides employers with retirement and benefits solutions for their employees. Its customer service vision is *providing better outcomes*, with the ultimate goal of providing the best customer service in the financial services industry. Like Cars.com, Fidelity's Workplace Solutions division sets goals for key customer service metrics, but those goals are only part of the story.

The division has something called a Voice of the Customer Ambassador program that's a cross-functional team of employees tasked with finding ways to continuously improve service and inspiring other employees to do the same. Ambassadors are nominated by senior managers and serve on the committee for 18 months. They're expected to spend eight to 12 hours each month working on customer service improvement projects.

One of the things the team is most known for is "busting rocks." A "rock" is the internal term used for issues that contribute to poor customer service or experiences. Voice of the Customer Ambassadors combine data from multiple sources to identify rocks, prioritize the biggest rocks, and then work with other employees across the division's seven locations to find solutions.

Bill Schimikowski, the Vice President of Customer Experience for Workplace Solutions, explains that the Ambassadors are deliberately chosen from multiple functions so they represent all aspects of the operation. According to Schimikowski, this helps the team reach across corporate silos that might otherwise prevent progress. "It's easy to blame legal when we can't do something that would benefit our customer," he says, "but when you have a lawyer on the Customer Ambassador team, that person can see both sides of the issue and propose a workable solution."

Organizations like Cars.com and Fidelity Investments aren't satisfied with simply achieving a certain customer satisfaction score. These organizations get their employees obsessed with customer service by setting lofty expectations for customer service, and then use data to find ways to continuously improve. Leaders in these companies also understand the danger in focusing too much on making metrics look good without understanding that the ultimate goal is to serve customers in a way that aligns with the customer service vision.

WHAT CAN HAPPEN WHEN GOALS DON'T ALIGN WITH YOUR VISION

Companies almost always create goals around customer service metrics. They set targets for average survey scores, speed of service, and even how closely employees adhere to their work schedule. The underlying management philosophy is that goals provide clarity and motivation: clarity by defining the outcomes they're expected to achieve, and motivation because people are generally motivated to put in extra effort when they have goals in front of them.

The trick lies in getting those goals to align with the customer service vision. Otherwise, goals can influence employee behavior in undesirable ways: employees may do something to achieve the goal that's not aligned with their company's customer service vision.

Employees in one company are expected to achieve a 95 percent average on a satisfaction survey sent to customers after they finished an interaction via phone, email, or chat. They're paid a monthly bonus when they achieve the goal, which is intended to be a healthy incentive for them to provide great service. Unfortunately, it also incentivizes these individuals to game the system to their advantage.

Here's what sometimes happens when a member of the frontline team assists a customer who seems upset. The customer service rep knows that if he continues helping her, she might give him an "unsatisfied" ranking on the survey, which could jeopardize his monthly bonus. He also knows he has the option of transferring the customer to an escalations team that handles upset customers and tricky situations. Transferring the customer means he avoids getting a bad survey, while his coworker on another team gets stuck cleaning up the mess.

The manager of the escalations team explained to me how the 95 percent customer satisfaction goal was actually demotivating to her team. She said achieving the goal was easy for the frontline team that primarily handled customer inquiries. A customer would contact the company, ask the customer service rep a simple question, and get a survey to ask if they were satisfied with the response. Achieving the 95 percent goal was almost a foregone conclusion.

The escalations team had it much harder because they worked with customers who were unsatisfied with the initial response they received and wanted to talk to someone with more technical knowledge or more authority. These customers were upset to begin with, which makes them predisposed to giving lower survey scores. Plus, members of the frontline team would often transfer upset callers unnecessarily to avoid lowering their own scores, which meant the escalations team had it even tougher.

This structure all but ensured the escalations team would never achieve the 95 percent target. Meanwhile, their counterparts on the frontline team received their bonuses every month. It seems unfair to judge the escalations team by the same goal as the other teams, but that's exactly what that company did.

Some organizations set customer service goals without a clear understanding of how the goals could drive behavior. One customer service leader I interviewed told me that her company surveys its customers and then reports the average score to senior management on a monthly basis. That was the extent of how the business used that data. Senior management might make a comment or two about the way the scores were trending compared to the previous month, but absolutely nothing would be done. Apparently this isn't unusual—an industry analyst I know estimates that just 10 percent of companies use their customer service survey data to actually improve service.

That's the inherent problem with relying solely on metrics without connecting them to the customer service vision. Heather Rattin and her team at Cars.com understand this challenge, so they combine metrics with other sources of data, such as the specific reasons customers need support, to tell a more complete story. Her goal is always to fulfill the customer service vision of *empowering the people we serve to act with conviction and navigate their world successfully.* This approach is unusual, as the vast majority of customer service leaders I speak to just look at data points without digging deeper to understand what can be done to improve.

Survey begging is another type of bad behavior that can happen when employees get too focused on the goal and lose sight of the customer service vision. This term describes a situation in which an employee asks a customer to give a positive score on a survey by explaining how it will directly benefit the customer, the employee, or both. Some employees offer discounts or even free merchandise in exchange for a good score. Other employees try to pull on their customers' heartstrings by explaining that they'll get in trouble if they don't maintain a high average.

Many employees who beg for survey scores have admitted to me that they're selective about the customers they ask to rate them. Unsurprisingly, they focus on the ones they perceive will give them a good rating. Retail employees might use a pen to circle the survey invitation on bottom of a customer's receipt and write their name next to it while encouraging the customer to fill it out. On the other hand, if a customer appears to be upset or grumpy, the employee might tear the survey invitation off the bottom of that customer's receipt so they don't risk getting a bad score.

There are plenty of other poor behaviors that come from employees who are overly goal focused. For instance, technical support teams often have targets for how quickly they can close out support tickets. Employees on these teams make their numbers look good by cherry-picking issues they know can be resolved faster. If they encounter a difficult issue, they'll close the ticket and mark it as resolved without verifying that the issue is actually fixed. This forces customers to open a new support ticket to get their issue handled. It's an annoying extra step for the customer, but it starts the clock anew for the employees with a support ticket closing speed goal.

In some cases, employees have even falsified data to achieve their customer service goals. For instance, employees at one business submitted fake surveys in an effort to inflate their overall customer satisfaction rating. Another company caught employees creating loyalty program accounts for fake customers to help them achieve their goals for loyalty program registrations. At Wells Fargo, a company we'll learn more about in Chapter 10, employees created over two million phony bank and credit card accounts in an effort to meet aggressive sales targets.

All these problems happen when customer service leaders set goals that cause employees to lose sight of the company's customer service vision. They're bad goals because they encourage bad behavior.

Bad goals have three distinct characteristics:

1. They divert attention away from the customer service vision.
2. They reward individualism.
3. They rely on extrinsic motivation.

Let's look back at the company that paid a bonus for maintaining a 95 percent survey average. Customer service leaders inadvertently encouraged poor behavior because they created a bad goal: *Customer Service Representatives who earn a satisfied rating on 95 percent or more of their customer service surveys each month will receive a $100 bonus.*

The cash bonus for achieving the 95 percent average focuses employees on achieving the score, but not necessarily delighting customers in the process. Since the bonus is paid individually, employees are encouraged to fend for themselves by transferring angry customers to someone else, even if it might hurt the team and the customer. And the cash bonus is an extrinsic, or external, motivator, which means employees are serving customers to earn cash, rather than because they're passionate about helping people.

Companies with strong customer service cultures still set goals for their employees. The difference is that they never lose sight of the customer service vision. Metrics such as survey score averages are helpful performance indicators, but only if the data are primarily used to find ways to continuously improve.

How to Set Good Customer Service Goals

This section of the chapter will provide you with step-by-step guidance for setting good customer service goals. We'll look at the criteria that make a goal good, the SMART model for setting clear goals, and important considerations when communicating goals to your team. You can also download a goal-setting worksheet here: www.servicculturebook.com/tools.

Good Goal Criteria

Good goals have three distinct characteristics that are the opposite of bad goals:

1. They focus attention on the customer service vision.
2. They reward teamwork.
3. They rely on intrinsic motivation.

Remember the bad goal example from earlier in the chapter? *Customer Service Representatives who earn a satisfied rating on 95 percent or more of their customer service surveys each month with receive a $100 bonus.*

Here's an example of what that 95 percent goal might look like if we re-wrote it using the good goal characteristics: *We will earn a satisfied rating on 95 percent of our customer service surveys this month.*

The first element of a good goal, focusing attention on the customer service vision, is admittedly tricky. A customer service team could easily fall into the trap of focusing on getting a good score, rather than using the survey as a tool for continuous improvement. This is where a strong leader can set the tone.

Heather Rattin and her customer service team at Cars.com review survey comments on a daily basis. They've made a habit of looking beyond the score to find out what their customers are really thinking. This daily communication focuses them on finding ways to serve their customers better, rather than on getting a better score. The score is just one indicator of how well they're doing; the focus is on continuous improvement that really has an impact.

The second element of a good goal is rewarding teamwork. Multiple employees often need to work together to deliver outstanding customer service. For example, in a typical restaurant, the host, server, busser, and chef all have an impact on customer satisfaction. Team-oriented goals encourage everyone to work together and help each other out.

In one organization I worked with, the escalations team shared the same customer service goal as the first tier team. This caused the first tier team and the escalations team to work together to *prevent* customers from getting transferred. For example, they made a list of the top 10 problems that caused calls to be transferred to escalations and identified several which could be handled by the first tier team if they only had a little more information. This allowed the first tier team to solve more problems quickly. It also freed up the escalations team to spend more time on the truly challenging issues. The result for the entire group was improved customer satisfaction.

The third element of a good goal is relying on intrinsic motivation. This means that employees are internally motivated to achieve the goal. They believe in the goal and what it stands for, and they're willing to do what it takes to get there.

There's a fundamental truth here that many business leaders fail to realize: most customer service professionals genuinely want to help their customers. I've spoken with thousands of customer service employees and have seen this common theme: setting a customer service goal and then working together as a team to achieve it causes motivation to soar.

Of course, surveys are just one example of a way to measure customer service. There are many other metrics that can be used. Here are a few examples:

- Customer retention
- Word-of-mouth referrals
- Ratings on external review sites
- First contact resolution
- Average response time (emails, chat, social media, etc.)

I liken these metrics to the gauges on a car's dashboard. Achieving a certain speed, holding the engine at a specific rate of revolutions per minute, or maintaining a particular fuel level isn't the objective. Instead, these gauges all tell you part of the story about how the car is performing and provide an early warning signal if something goes wrong. The real goal, of course, is reaching your destination. In customer service, the destination that customer-focused companies are constantly heading toward is their customer service vision.

Involving employees in the goal-setting process is one additional element of a good goal that's not an absolute requirement, but it is a best practice. This gives people a greater sense of ownership for the goal since they helped set it. Getting employee feedback up front can also help you identify situations when a goal might not be achievable.

The SMART Goals Model

Those three elements of a good goal are a great starting point, but customer service goals should also follow the SMART model. There are a few different versions of the SMART model for setting goals, but here's my preferred version:

- S = Specific
- M = Measurable
- A = Attainable
- R = Relevant
- T = Time-Bound

You can find a SMART goals worksheet at www.serviceculturebook.com/tools.

Companies often set vague customer service goals that are difficult to define and measure. For example, I've seen more than one company set this goal as part of their strategic plan: *Improve customer service.*

The challenge with a goal like this is it's hard to know what exactly needs to be improved. Nobody can say for sure how we're doing now, what needs to change, nor whether the goal has been achieved.

A SMART goal provides a much clearer blueprint to follow. *We will achieve a satisfied rating on 95 percent of our customer service surveys this month.*

Let's take a look at how this fits the SMART model.

We know it fits three of the criteria right away. It's specific because it focuses on the customer service survey. The goal can be measured by counting the percentage of surveys with a satisfied rating. It's also time-bound because we've set the end of the month as the deadline for achieving this goal.

Some context is required to know if the goal fits the other two criteria. You don't know if it's attainable without knowing the current survey results and what needs to be done to achieve the 95 percent result. You might be on track if last month's result was 94 percent; you might be wildly off base if your previous score was 72 percent.

It's also hard to know if the goal is relevant without comparing it to the customer service vision. Goals for customer satisfaction scores are typically relevant, but many companies also set goals that aren't directly relevant to outstanding service. Examples include productivity goals, goals for complying with company policy, and even attendance goals.

COMMUNICATING GOALS TO THE TEAM

SMART goals that meet the good goal criteria can help motivate customer-obsessed employees. The key is that employees need to be aware of the goals and understand how close they are to achieving them. It's the responsibility of customer service leaders to ensure this happens.

First, you'll need a scoreboard. This is something that allows employees to easily access customer service objectives and results. It could be an electronic display, a physical bulletin board, or something employees can access on their computers.

One manager I know used a bulletin board to inform employees about the score for secret shopper reports. The team's goal was to average an 85 percent score on secret shopper reports each month, so the manager attached a string horizontally across the middle of the board and put a sign on the string that read "85%." As secret shopper reports came in, the manager would either pin a copy of the report above or below the line, depending on the score. Employees could quickly see how they were doing in comparison to the goal and review any report that fell short of the target.

The next thing you'll need is a regular announcement. This is a formal reminder to employees about the goal and the results they've achieved. It could be shared in an email update, a monthly newsletter, or in a presentation from a customer service leader.

The rule of thumb is to share this information as often as you would any other vital business information. So if you update the company on financial performance once per month, it's a good idea to do the same for customer service. Providing regular, formal updates helps establish customer service as an important aspect of business performance.

The third part of your goal communication strategy is regular informal communication from customer service leaders. Think of this as a coach sharing updates with an athletic team and helping the athletes adjust accordingly. This includes one-on-one meetings, informal emails, and informal team meetings.

Let's go back to Cars.com. Rattin and her managers share customer service survey results with their teams on a daily basis. That means employees are receiving constant, consistent updates about what's going well and what needs some extra attention.

I have one last reminder about customer service goals. Whatever metric or metrics you choose to measure customer service, make sure employees don't get so fixated on achieving a score that they lose sight of the customer service vision. The metrics are meant to help you measure progress rather than being the definition of success.

Goals help customer service leaders and employees alike assess what's working well and where there are opportunities for improvement. That's because customer-focused organizations never settle for good enough. These companies are constantly trying to find ways to make their customer service even better.

NOTES:

36 Jeanette Cooper, "Digital Air Strike Releases 2015 Social Media Trends Study for the Automotive Industry," *Digital Air Strike*, November 3, 2015. http://digitalairstrike.com/digital-air-strike-releases-2015-social-media-trends-study-for-the-automotive-industry/.

CHAPTER 7

Hiring Employees Who Will Embrace Your Culture

AT FIRST GLANCE, PUBLIX SEEMS like an ordinary supermarket. There's a produce section, a bakery, and aisles filled with packaged food. The checkout stands are near the front.

Yet everything feels just a little different. There's a large, welcoming customer service desk near the front entrance. The aisles are wider than a typical supermarket. The restrooms are clean. The produce section even has signs describing how to select, store, and prepare various fruits and vegetables.

You might also notice the employees. They're outgoing, friendly, and helpful—and there are lots of them. It seems like there's someone ready to help everywhere you turn in the store.

The supermarket industry as a whole enjoys high customer service rankings on sites like the Temkin Ratings and the American Customer Satisfaction Index. Publix is at the very top. In 2016, it was the top-rated supermarket chain in the Temkin Customer Service Ratings (#2 among all businesses) and the top-rated company in any industry in the Temkin Customer Experience Ratings.[37] Publix also earned the #3 ranking among supermarket chains on the American Customer Satisfaction Index for 2016. That same year, MSN named the company "America's Favorite Supermarket."[38]

Publix has developed a strong, customer-focused culture by following many of the same steps as other organizations profiled in this book. The company has a clear customer service vision, *Where Shopping is a Pleasure,* that guides all aspects of the business including strategic decisions, store layouts, and employee training. Its leaders work hard to engage employees with the customer-focused culture by providing ongoing training and recognizing them for emulating company values.

Above all, Publix does exceptionally well in hiring the right people. The company builds and sustains a customer service culture by consistently hiring employees who have a passion for delivering the type of service for which Publix is known.

How Publix Hires for Culture Fit

Customer service isn't a job that's right for everyone. The qualities we expect in a customer service professional, such as friendliness, helpfulness, and empathy, don't come naturally for many people. That's why companies need to be picky about who they hire for customer-facing roles.

Imagine hiring an employee for Publix, a company offering world-class customer service. An average employee won't do. You need someone with extraordinary people skills—someone who enthusiastically embraces the *Where Shopping is a Pleasure* customer service vision.

Hiring managers at Publix don't need to find just one extraordinary employee. The chain has more than 1,000 stores spread across six states in the Southeastern United States. This means it must employ thousands of outstanding customer service professionals who fit in with the company's customer-focused culture. To address this challenge, Publix created a selection process that helps it recruit the right employees.

This selection process begins with a culture page on the company's website that provides job candidates with extensive details about what it's like to work at Publix. The page includes information about the company's mission and values, testimonials from happy employees, job descriptions for open positions, career paths highlighting advancement opportunities, and tips for applying for a job. This makes it easy for prospective job applicants to see if Publix is an organization they'd enjoy working for. (See for yourself at http:// corporate.publix.com/careers.)

Internally, the company defines the qualities of an ideal employee to make the selection process easier for hiring managers to make consistent hiring decisions. Marcy Hamrick, its Manager of Talent Acquisition, lists the top three[39]:

1. Driven by a need to serve others
2. Passionate about working together as a team
3. Capable of great attention to detail

The company's carefully-designed employee selection process helps hiring managers evaluate applicants for these qualities. For example, job applicants who are granted an interview are asked to prepare a short statement describing how they can help Publix deliver outstanding customer service. Candidates are asked to deliver their statement at the start of the interview. The interviewer uses the content of the statement to help assess whether the applicant is *driven by a need to serve others.*

Publix has another unusual twist in its selection process. In an age of online job applications, people who wish to work in a Publix store (versus in a corporate role) must apply in person. Each store has a kiosk near the front where people can browse through open positions and complete a job application.

Instructions on the Publix website make it clear that job applicants for in-store positions are encouraged to seek out employees with questions about the working environment or the application process when they come into a store to apply for a job. Whether or not a candidate uses this opportunity to engage with potential coworkers is a way of testing whether the person is *passionate about working together as a team.*

Yet another element in the selection process is how the candidate prepares for an interview. The company's career page offers a list of interviewing tips to help job seekers put their best foot forward. One tip advises candidates to thank the hiring manager at the end of the interview, and then to ask when a decision will be made. Another tip advises candidates to bring appropriate work samples, so a person applying for a cake decorator position might bring pictures of cakes they've decorated. Observing whether candidates follow these interviewing tips is a good way for hiring managers to determine if the candidate is *capable of great attention to detail.*

Publix also uses behavioral interviews as part of its selection process. A behavioral interview consists of a set of questions that focus on an applicant's prior experience. For example, an interviewer might ask a prospective employee to describe a situation when he or she served an angry customer. Asking for specifics requires the candidate to look beyond hypothetical examples and share a real story. The interviewer can use the response to assess whether the candidate could easily recall a relevant example, and if the candidate described an appropriate course of action.

Another essential aspect of hiring for culture fit is the company's promote-from-within philosophy. Publix tries to hire internal candidates for leadership positions whenever possible, because these employees tend to have a firm grasp of the company culture and have demonstrated their ability to model it for the people on their team. For instance, Todd Jones, the company's CEO, joined Publix in 1980 as a bagger; he spent the next 36 years working his way up, and became CEO in early 2016.

This focus on hiring people who embrace the company culture is a key trait shared by many customer-focused companies. Rackspace hires people who come from professions like hospitality that require a lot of empathy, based on the company's belief that technical skills can easily be taught, but empathy is much harder to develop. Shake Shack recognizes that its promote-from-within philosophy is an essential part of maintaining the chain's *Stand For Something Good* culture as the company grows.

Clio, a company you'll meet in Chapter 8, gives job applicants a sample customer email and asks them to write a response. This simple test gauges several qualities that are part of Clio's company culture.

1. Applicants must be resourceful enough to find the answer to the customer's question (the answers can be found on its website).
2. They must be able to write a response that's easy to understand.
3. They must demonstrate the ability to use their personality to connect with the customer via a brief email.

It's a tall order, and not everyone can do it, but that's what makes this test an effective way to screen for candidates who will fit in with the company's customer-focused culture.

Many organizations use product advocacy as a way of screening job candidates for culture fit. The idea is to hire employees who are already passionate about the company's products or services. For example, many people who work at REI are outdoor enthusiasts who view the job as an opportunity to support their passion through discounts on equipment and clothing, the opportunity to lead classes, or the chance to share their enthusiasm with others.

Just one good hire can make a big difference in a company's or team's culture. One client I worked with sold accessories for boats, RVs, and golf carts. The company had a small team of support professionals who answered phone calls and emails from customers. None of the support team members were particularly enthusiastic about boating, RVing, or golfing, so they sometimes had a challenge connecting with their customers. This changed, however, when the company hired a new employee who was an avid boater. The new employee shared her personal knowledge with her coworkers, which helped them understand their products better. This, in turn, led to an increase in sales as everyone on the team was more able to enthusiastically help customers to confidently make a purchasing decision.

What Happens When You Hire Employees Who Don't Fit Your Company's Culture

Customer-focused companies like Publix build and sustain a customer-focused culture by hiring people who are already obsessed with providing their unique brand of customer service. But what can happen if a company hires people who don't fit the company's culture?

One small company hired a customer service representative named Brandon, a recent high school graduate who had no previous work experience and no real ambition. This wasn't the typical profile for a successful employee, but he was hired anyway at the owner's insistence. Brandon happened to be dating the owner's daughter, and he wanted to give Brandon an opportunity. (Or perhaps he wanted to keep a close eye on his daughter's boyfriend!)

Brandon immediately clashed with the customer service team's culture. The rest of the team had a great deal of enthusiasm for helping customers and enjoyed learning the intricacies of each new product line. Brandon, on the other hand, had no enthusiasm for serving others and little interest in learning about the company's products.

Brandon's coworkers began to bristle at how his laziness created extra work for them. For instance, he frequently promised customers that he would fix a problem, but then neglected to follow through and resolve the issue. The customer would inevitably call back angry at the lack of a resolution, and another customer service rep would have to bear the brunt of it.

The rest of the customer service team was relieved when Brandon quit after just a few months on the job. The customer service manager was relieved, too, since the owner had vetoed any corrective action the manager had suggested to address Brandon's poor performance.

Unfortunately, the customer service team now had a lingering mistrust toward management for allowing someone who was so obviously not a fit to remain part of the team.

This case may be a little extreme, but it illustrates three of the problems caused by poor hiring decisions:

1. Poor customer service
2. Reduced morale
3. Increased turnover

It's difficult to provide outstanding customer service when employees lack enthusiasm for helping others or have no affinity for their company's products or services. The sporting goods retailer Sports Authority went out of business in 2016 after being plagued by a variety of problems, including poor customer service and disengaged employees. If you visited Sports Authority to buy camping gear, you'd likely be greeted by an employee whose helpfulness consisted of pointing to the camping section from across the store. Contrast this with the same shopping trip at REI, where you'd more likely be served by an associate who was an avid camper and genuinely enjoyed helping others gear up for a successful camping trip of their own.

Morale also suffers when poor hiring decisions are made. New employees disturb team unity when they don't embrace the culture. Their inability or unwillingness to serve customers creates extra work for other employees, who usually resent having to go out of their way to clean up a co-worker's mess. Stress levels rise, too: a 2016 study of contact center agents found that 36 percent of agents who faced a high risk of burnout felt they could not rely on their co-workers to deliver outstanding customer service.[40]

Turnover is perhaps the easiest-to-measure problem caused by poor hiring. A study by the Center for American Progress estimated that replacing an employee can cost an average of 20 percent of an employee's annual salary for employees who make $50,000 or less per year.[41] To put that in perspective, the average annual wage for a customer service employee in the United States is approximately $27,000.[42] Replacing that employee costs $5,400, assuming the 20 percent replacement cost average.

What goes into that $5,400 figure? It includes increased wages and overtime needed to cover shifts for the lost employee, recruiting expenses (advertising, interviewing, background checks, drug screening, etc.), training costs, new equipment (tools, uniforms, etc.), and administrative costs. You can calculate the cost of turnover for employees in your organization or on your customer service team using the turnover calculator found here: www.servicecluturebook.com/tools.

High turnover plagues many industries employing lots of customer service workers. Contact centers regularly experience annual turnover rates of 20 percent or higher. Retail stores often face turnover rates of 50 percent or more. Hospitality industries, such as restaurants, can see as many as 70 percent of their employees leave each year.

It's incredibly difficult to sustain company culture in a business where there's a revolving door of employees.

So why do some companies consistently hire the wrong employees? Some managers grow tired of the extra work caused by being short-staffed and simply rush to hire someone without thoroughly vetting their qualifications. Other managers don't know how to select the right employees. In many cases, there's no company-wide consensus on what qualities make a job applicant a good fit with the culture.

Some organizations try to address these issues by creating a structured process to recruit and select new hires. Unfortunately, a hiring process won't guarantee that you'll hire stellar employees. There's often one of three flaws standing in the way.

The first flaw is emphasizing experience when recruiting job candidates. Recruiters look for people who have previously worked in jobs similar to the one for which they're hiring. The theory is that people with similar experience will have developed easily-transferrable skills.

The problem with this approach is that not all experience is necessarily good experience. An employee may have learned bad habits from a previous employer, especially if that company wasn't customer-focused. Or the job candidate might be leaving a previous job because he or she wasn't a very good employee; if so, they'll likely struggle in the new job too.

The second flaw in many hiring processes is focusing too much on skills. Skills are necessary in almost every job, whether it's an interpersonal skill like empathizing with customers, or a technical skill like the ability to troubleshoot a software program. However, having the right skills doesn't mean an employee will be a fit with the company culture. For instance, many people know how to work as a cashier and ring up customer transactions, but there are many dour, surly cashiers who would immediately clash with the customer-focused culture at a company like Publix.

The third flaw is trying to hire for culture fit without clearly defining what that means. Leaders often make the mistake of using their gut feeling in an interview to determine if a prospective employee has the proper attitude and will fit in well with the team. What these leaders end up doing is hiring people like themselves. A 2012 study by three researchers at the University of Pennsylvania—Jason Dana, Robyn M. Dawes, and Nathanial R. Peterson—revealed that just asking random questions to assess a candidate's future performance actually results in worse hiring decisions than if the candidate hadn't been interviewed at all![43]

Rene was an area director for a company with locations throughout the country. Her company had a well-defined process for hiring customer service employees, but she also had the autonomy to make the ultimate hiring decision for employees in her area. Although Rene had a bubbly personality, she tended to be disorganized and unfocused. When it came to hiring employees, she routinely hired individuals who had bubbly personalities but were disorganized and unfocused, just like her. These hires clashed with the company's hiring profile that called for organized, conscientious employees who could anticipate customer needs and resolve issues before they happened. Hiring employees who didn't fit with the company culture ultimately cost Rene her job when her area's performance couldn't keep up with the high standards expected throughout the company.

Adam Grant, author of *Originals: How Non-Conformists Move the World*, told *Forbes Magazine*, "Emphasizing cultural fit leads you to bring in a bunch of people who think in similar ways to your existing employees."[44] His point was that hiring people based on an arbitrary assessment of fit can lead to stagnation. Instead, Grant suggested that companies should hire based on what a potential employee can contribute to the culture. Healthy teams have a diversity of perspectives, personalities, and skills that complement each other.

Hiring without regard for culture fit is dangerous – but going by gut instinct to hire for fit can be just as dangerous. So what should organizational leaders do to hire the right employees to serve their customers? The answer lies in having a well-designed hiring process.

How to Hire for Culture Fit

Publix and other organizations with strong, customer-focused cultures have a process in place to screen job applicants for both skills and culture fit. The actual process varies from organization to organization, but there are three general steps:

1. Create an Ideal Candidate Profile
2. Design test to find Ideal Candidates
3. Commit to the process

Step 1: Create an Ideal Candidate Profile

It's helpful to think of an Ideal Candidate Profile as an enhanced job description.

Job descriptions typically outline the key responsibilities, as well as the skills and qualifications required to be successful in a given position. Many companies use job descriptions as a guide when hiring employees.

An Ideal Candidate Profile takes this a step further by highlighting the characteristics an employee should possess that would make him or her a good fit with the company culture. It also separates the qualities a job applicant *must* have to be hired from those that would be *nice* for the applicant to have, but which they could also develop through training.

The reason for separating the Must-Haves from the Nice-to-Haves is what recruiters call the Purple Squirrel Problem. There are a lot of things that are purple and there are a lot of squirrels. But it's very difficult to find a purple squirrel! In recruiting, this means it's difficult to find the perfect employee with every desirable quality. The more Must-Haves that are listed on your Ideal Candidate Profile, the harder it is to find that person. Prioritizing your Must-Haves will help you focus on what you really need.

You can create an Ideal Candidate Profile by separating job qualifications into these categories:

- Organizational Must-Haves
- Organizational Nice-to-Haves
- Job-Specific Must-Haves
- Job-Specific Nice-to-Haves

The Organizational Must-Haves category includes qualities that describe an employee who is a good fit with your company's organizational culture. An employee needs to possess these qualities regardless of their role within the organization. At Publix, for example, all new hires are required to be "driven by a need to serve others," no matter whether they work in the bakery department, the produce department, or in a corporate role.

The Organizational Nice-to-Haves category consists of qualities that would be nice for a new employee to possess, but aren't required. These qualities might be used to make a final hiring decision if one qualified candidate has a few more Nice-to-Haves than another, but the company is also willing to hire a new employee who doesn't have them. For instance, Publix looks for job applicants who are current or former employees because it has a hire-from-within strategy, but external candidates are also considered.

The Job-Specific Must-Haves category is composed of qualifications a person needs to be considered for a specific job. For example, an applicant must have prior experience as a Meat Cutter or Meat Cutter Apprentice to apply for a Meat Cutter position at a Publix store. A person who lacks the experience of being a Meat Cutter but is still interested in working as one would be encouraged to apply for a Meat Cutter Apprentice role, since that position doesn't require prior experience.

Finally, the Job-Specific Nice-to-Haves category is, like the organizational Nice-to-Haves, composed of qualifications that might break a tie between two qualified candidates, but are not absolutely required. For instance, a Meat Cutter Apprentice working at Publix might have a leg up on a job applicant with meat cutting experience at another grocery chain, but working as a *Publix* Meat Cutter Apprentice isn't a Must-Have qualification to become a Publix Meat Cutter.

In my experience helping clients create Ideal Candidate Profiles, the biggest challenge is separating the Must-Have qualities from Nice-to-Haves. A good test to see if something is truly a Must-Have is to compare your existing employees to your Ideal Candidate Profile. If a successful employee lacks a Must-Have quality (or lacked it when he or she was first hired), then you know that quality isn't truly a Must-Have.

Figure 7.1 contains a sample Ideal Candidate Profile for a tasting room host at a fictitious winery, Sunny Hills Vineyard. I've also created an Ideal Candidate Profile worksheet you can download and use to create your own profiles: www.servicebookculturebook.com/tools.

Figure 7.1: Ideal Candidate Profile

Organization: Sunny Hills Vineyard
Position: Tasting Room Host

Customer Service Vision: *We make it fun to discover great wine.*

Organizational Must-Haves

- Enthusiasm for wine
- Continuous learner
- Team player

Organizational Nice-to-Haves

- Understanding of the wine industry
- General knowledge of common wine varietals
- Familiarity with the unique characteristics of our winery's growing region

Job-Specific Must-Haves

- A passion for teaching others about wine
- Ability to develop rapport with guests
- Capable of clear and confident communication

Job-Specific Nice-to-Haves

- Introductory Sommelier certification (or similar)
- Current TIPS certification card
- Previous winery experience

Here's another tip that can help you save some time. Once you create your first Ideal Candidate Profile, you can use it as a template to create profiles for other positions. The first two categories, Organizational Must-Haves and Organizational Nice-to-Haves, should stay the same for each position, so half the work is already done.

Step Two: Design Tests to Find Ideal Candidates

Once you create an Ideal Candidate Profile for a position, you need to design a screening process that tests for each quality in the profile, indicating whether job applicants fit those particular qualifications. To do this, take each item in your Ideal Candidate Profile and determine how you'll tell whether or not a job applicant possesses that quality.

These tests are the basis of your candidate screening process.

As an example, think about what you might see on a candidate's resume or job application that could indicate a good fit with your organization. A nonprofit that runs music programs for children has applicants list hobbies and interests on their job application. The recruiter looks for applicants who play an instrument, sing, or have an avid interest in music, because people who have a strong connection to music are much more likely to relate to the music program participants than people who don't share that passion.

The interview is another important opportunity to test job applicants for culture fit. The key is to use what's called a *structured interview*, where every applicant for the same position is asked the same standard set of questions. Each question should connect to at least one quality on your Ideal Candidate Profile for that role.

Let's say you manage a tasting room at a winery and want to hire tasting room hosts who are passionate about teaching guests about wine. You might test job applicants for this quality by asking each person to share an experience they had where they learned something about wine that most consumers don't know. A good response would be a story where the job applicant spent time learning about wine and could relate what they learned in a clear and easily-understood manner.

Many recruiters limit themselves to looking at just three sources of information: the candidate's job application, their resume, and their responses to interview questions. These are all helpful, but there's no reason to limit yourself to just these three! A well-structured selection process can test a candidate's qualifications in a wide variety of ways.

One of my clients created an Ideal Candidate Profile for employees working in the parking department on a college campus. They wanted people who could anticipate potential problems and plan ahead to avoid them. The way they tested job applicants for this quality was subtle, but effective.

When a recruiter scheduled an interview with a job applicant, the recruiter did not volunteer to give the applicant directions to the parking office. (Like many college campuses, finding parking and then navigating to a specific office was difficult.) Successful applicants did one of two things. Some would ask the recruiter for directions, in which case the recruiter readily provided the requested information. Others went on the school's website to research transportation options, parking locations, and estimate the amount of travel time required.

Unsuccessful applicants arrived late for the interview. They would tell the recruiter they couldn't find parking or got lost trying to find the office. No matter the excuse, it was a good test to show the applicant didn't naturally anticipate a problem that plagued many visitors to the college campus.

I want to offer one word of caution about the candidate screening process. Successful candidates will generally be delighted to receive a job offer. But what about the people who aren't offered a job? In many cases, these people far outnumber the people who are hired. It's important to design a selection process that treats all candidates with dignity and respect. Companies frequently waste candidates' time with multiple steps that don't add value to the selection process. Some fail to notify rejected applicants of their status.

Keep in mind that all job applicants are potential customers. They might choose whether or not to do business with your company in the future based on their experience with the selection process. They may encourage or discourage friends and family members to apply for an open position based on their impression of your organizational culture. If at all possible, you want job applicants to love your organization even if they don't get to join it.

STEP THREE: COMMIT TO THE PROCESS

Impatience may be the biggest reason why companies fail to hire employees who fit their organizational culture. It takes time to create an Ideal Candidate Profile for each position. It takes more time to design a screening process that tests for each quality in the profile. And it takes guts to stick to the process.

Yet many businesses find themselves suddenly faced with an urgent need to hire customer service employees. A company might be opening a new location that needs to be staffed. A busy season might be approaching and extra employees will soon be needed. Or a key person may have left and must be urgently replaced.

All these circumstances create pressure on hiring managers to fill positions quickly. In doing so, they might be tempted to skip steps in the process and hire someone less qualified than would normally be considered for a position. The danger here is in hiring the wrong employee. Poor hiring decisions tend to have a cumulative effect on a manager's time. The employee needs more training. The manager has to fix the employee's mistakes. The rest of the team develops morale issues caused by an employee who doesn't fit in. Plus, the manager will soon need to hire and train yet another employee when the poor hire doesn't work out.

Companies with strong customer service cultures stay committed to their hiring process. Hiring great employees creates a self-reinforcing cycle for customer-focused companies. Your employees will deliver outstanding service, which makes a strong positive impression on your customers. Customers see your company as a great place to work, so more people apply who already love your brand. With more applicants, you can be even more selective about whom you hire.

NOTES:

37 The Temkin Group, "2016 Temkin Customer Service Ratings," *Temkin Ratings*, 2016. http://temkinratings.com/temkin-ratings/temkin-customer-service-ratings-2016/.

38 Janna Herron, "America's favorite supermarkets, ranked," *MSN*, July 18, 2016. http://www.msn.com/en-us/money/companies/americas-favorite-supermarkets-ranked/ss-BBu4jPa?li=BBnb7Kz#image=1.

39 Deena Shanker, "They're hiring! These great employers have 108,622 openings," *Fortune*, March 12, 2015. http://fortune.com/2015/03/05/best-companies-open-positions/.

40 Jeff Toister, "How to Battle Agent Burnout." *Toister Performance Solutions*, 2016: www.toistersolutions.com/burnout.

41 Heather Boushey and Sarah Jane Glynn, "There Are Significant Business Costs to Replacing Employees," *Center for American Progress*, November 16, 2012. https://www.americanprogress.org/wp-content/uploads/2012/11/CostofTurnover.pdf.

42 PayScale estimates the average hourly wage for a customer service employee in the U.S. is $13.01 per hour. This works out to $27,060.80 for an employee who averages 40 hours per week.

43 Jason Dana and Robyn M. Dawes, "Belief in the Unstructured Interview: The Persistence of an Illusion" (working paper) *University of Pennsylvania*, August 15, 2012. http://www.sas.upenn.edu/~danajd/interview.pdf.

44 Dan Schwabel, "Adam Grant: Why You Shouldn't Hire For Cultural Fit," *Forbes*, February 2, 2016. http://www.forbes.com/sites/danschawbel/2016/02/02/adam-grant-why-you-shouldnt-hire-for-cultural-fit/#2f71777c56f5.

CHAPTER 8

Training Employees to Embody Your Culture

A CUSTOMER CALLED CLIO'S SUPPORT team with a unique billing request. She wanted to pay by check even though the company's software is only set up to accept credit card payments.

Clio provides legal practice management software that helps lawyers run their law practices. The software is provided on a subscription basis, and customers are billed monthly or yearly to access it via the internet. The caller was a busy lawyer who didn't want to spend a lot of time dealing with support to get her issue resolved.

Support calls like this are a common challenge for many software companies. Customers often want special features or options that aren't available, and there's always a risk they'll take their business to a competitor if they can't get what they want.

Here's where support agents at a typical company simply tell their customer, "Sorry, but that option isn't available." Then it's up to the customer to decide if they want to keep their account anyway or take their business elsewhere.

Not at Clio. While the support agent was aware that paying by check wasn't an option, he didn't want to lose the customer's business. He knew that preventing churn (i.e., retaining customers) was a key part of the company's customer service vision: *Our goal is to help our customers succeed and realize the full value of our Product. This results in Evangelists and less Churn.*

The agent listened patiently to the lawyer's concerns, hoping to find a way to make her happy and convince her to keep her account. She explained she was used to paying for services by check and believed this was the simplest way for her to keep track of her expenses. This insight helped the support agent understand that the customer's real need was to keep things easy and spend as little time as possible managing her Clio account.

So he explained to her how automatic credit card billing was actually easier than paying by check. It would save her time since the payments were made automatically, and it would prevent any service disruptions since she wouldn't have to remember to mail a check each time her payment was due.

The customer was delighted by the end of the call. She felt like the support agent had listened to her concerns and understood her needs. Best of all, she kept her Clio account.

Daily customer interactions like this have helped Clio grow at a 40 percent rate annually. Most of that growth is driven by word-of-mouth referrals from happy customers who tell other lawyers about the company's excellent software and helpful service.

This outstanding service generates incredible customer loyalty. Clio's churn rate is just one percent, meaning that 99 out of 100 customers renew their subscriptions. The company's customer satisfaction ratings are consistently in the mid-90 percent range.

This isn't an accident. Clio's executives made a strategic choice to use service as a way to differentiate the company from the competition. A big part of this strategy is training all Clio employees to embody its service culture when assisting customers.

How Clio Trains Its Employees to Embody Its Culture

It's not enough to know what the vision says at Clio. Employees are expected to know what it means and be able to explain how it applies to them. To this end, they're given extensive and ongoing training to help them embody Clio's culture when serving customers.

Chapter 4 explained how to engage employees with your organization's customer service culture. In many ways, this process overlaps with training.

However, there's one key difference. *Engagement* is a process of cultivating employee attitudes so they believe in their company's customer service vision and want to use it as a guide in their daily work. *Training* provides employees with the specific knowledge, skills, and abilities to turn that desire into action.

Let's look at the example of Clio's customer support rep from the beginning of this chapter. He was *engaged* because he had a desire to apply the customer service vision of helping customers succeed in using Clio's software so they'd remain loyal. His *training* helped him in this quest. The customer support rep knew what payment methods were available and which were not. His rapport-building, active listening, and empathy skills allowed him to have a constructive dialogue with the customer about her reasons for wanting to pay by check. Finally, his ability to partner with this individual and propose an acceptable solution ultimately saved the account and created a happy and loyal customer.

Clio's customer support team receives a lot of training to reinforce the company's vision and develop their ability to embody it in the service they provide. New hires are introduced to the vision during their initial training. It's augmented with training videos from the online education company Lynda.com to help agents develop specific customer service skills like rapport building, active listening, and empathizing.

In addition, support agents receive ongoing training on how to actually execute the customer service vision. This includes one-on-one coaching from their supervisor to help develop their skills, regular team meetings to reinforce the vision, and performance feedback based on guidelines reflecting the vision. This constant training and reinforcement ensures that support agents never forget the role they play in Clio's customer service culture.

Training isn't limited to Clio's customer-facing support team. Employees in other departments receive training to ensure they understand the company's customer service philosophy. Rian Gauvreau, Clio's cofounder and Chief Operating Officer, wants all of the company's employees to see their job through the eyes of their customers.

"The way to solve for customer pain is to put your customer first," Gauvreau said. One of the ways employees learn to put the customer first is through what's called "support ride-alongs." This is where people from other parts of the company spend time working alongside support agents to solve customer issues. "It motivates the staff to know they're helping customers," Gauvreau explained.

The ride-alongs help employees better understand the issues customers face. For instance, if a product designer is working on a new feature, she can reflect on the time she spent doing a support ride-along to envision how that feature will look from a customer's perspective.

In addition, Clio hosts an annual user conference, giving employees the opportunity to meet customers face-to-face. User conferences are common for software companies. They gather existing and prospective clients for a few days of product training, best practice sharing, and user feedback sessions. These conferences are generally marketing initiatives aimed at increasing customer loyalty or enticing new clients. What makes Clio different is how they use this opportunity to help employees strengthen their customer focus.

For instance, each year, developers spend the first day of the conference gathering feedback and suggestions from customers in attendance. By day two, the company implements changes to the online software based on the feedback they received on day one! Making changes so quickly demonstrates the company's commitment to helping its customers succeed.

Another example of a culture training initiative at Clio was an exercise called "Know Our Customer." Every employee in the company participated (about 200 employees), with each person interviewing at least one customer. The goal was to create an opportunity for all employees to develop their empathy skills by spending time learning from a customer. As a result of this exercise, people in all departments were able to adopt a customer perspective when doing their jobs.

Training doesn't always have to be a formal process. In fact, most of the learning that occurs in the workplace happens through informal experiences. At Clio, this includes discussing and reinforcing customer focus in all-hands meetings and one-on-one conversations with a supervisor. The company also has a peer-recognition program where employees give each other kudos for a job well done. The only requirement is that the recognition must include a description of how the employee's actions aligned with being customer-focused.

Comprehensive and ongoing customer service training is a common characteristic among companies with strong service cultures. Zendesk (a company you'll meet in Chapter 12) has something similar to Clio's ride-along program, where employees who don't normally work in customer support spend time responding to customer issues. Shake Shack trains all its leaders to embody their *Stand For Something Good* philosophy and reinforce those values with their employees. JetBlue has all newly hired crewmembers (employees) attend a two-day orientation to learn about the company culture.

Leaders at customer-focused companies understand that employees can get lost without the right training and guidance.

What Can Happen If You Don't Provide Culture Training

Many companies fail to provide employees with specific training on how to embody the culture. This happens for a variety of reasons. In some organizations, leaders fail to recognize the need to give employees specific instructions on how to use the culture as a guide to serving customers. In other companies, leaders prefer to spend time on other work and don't make developing the culture a priority.

In one example, a customer service representative was asked to describe his company's customer service philosophy. He knew the company had a set of five core values, but he struggled to come up with an answer.

The rep knew the five core values were supposed to represent how people should interact with customers, coworkers, and other important stakeholders. There was a sign displaying these values in front of the building where he worked, and another sign hung within sight of his cubicle. He even had a mug on his desk with the five values written on it, which he'd been given at a meeting where the values were announced.

What this employee didn't know was what the values meant, or how they applied to his daily work. He'd never received any training on this, and his boss never discussed the values with the team.

The five values were crafted by the company's corporate communications team after months of deliberation, focus groups, and word-smithing sessions with senior leaders. They sounded good, but they did nothing to guide employees' actions.

When employees aren't trained on their company's customer service culture, employees can't consciously use the culture to guide their actions. Furthermore, individual employees, different departments, and various company locations are likely to develop their own interpretations of the customer service philosophy that might or might not complement one another.

Some companies attempt to train employees on the customer service culture, but there isn't full commitment. Many organizations rely on a single learning event such as a big kick-off party or a one-time training session. The initial excitement quickly fades as these companies fail to constantly and consistently reinforce the culture through multiple training programs and ongoing informal learning opportunities.

The challenge with training through just a single event is that most information is stored in our brains on a "use it or lose it" basis. For example, you probably had a combination locker in high school. Most of us could open that locker in just a few seconds back when we used it on a daily basis. But what would happen if you stood in front of that same locker today? Even assuming the combination hadn't changed, most people wouldn't be able to open it. The combination you used to recall instantly has long been forgotten because you stopped using it.

When I worked for a parking management company, all new employees learned about the company's customer service vision in a new hire orientation session organized by my corporate training department. My team was also responsible for conducting site audits at our various locations to evaluate customer service. One of the items on the audit was spot-checking employees to see if they could describe the customer service vision.

The results varied widely. At high-performing locations, employees typically had the customer service vision memorized. They could describe what it meant and explain how they used it as a guide when serving customers. These employees remembered the vision not just from their new hire orientation, but also from frequent discussions with their boss and signs displaying the vision that hung at their parking facility. They also attended the company's annual customer service refresher training where they were reminded about the vision.

The audit results were very different at our locations with poor customer service performance. Here, most employees had forgotten what they learned about the customer service vision in their new hire orientation by the time their location was audited. Their manager didn't discuss it with them, the vision wasn't displayed anywhere at their location, and they didn't attend the annual refresher training.

Other companies do a great job of training and reinforcing their customer service vision among customer-facing employees, but they don't do the same thing for employees working in other departments. This creates a disconnect between employees who view themselves in customer service and those who don't.

All employees are ultimately connected to customer service in some way, whether directly or indirectly. A restaurant server is obviously in customer service because he or she has direct and frequent contact with guests. But what about the chef? A guest's satisfaction will be affected by whether the chef cooks the meal properly or honors special requests. How about the dishwasher? This person may never interact directly with a guest, but a guests' experience will certainly be impacted by whether or not the dishes are clean.

The IT support manager for a major retail chain described the danger of not viewing certain departments as essential to customer service. "Our stores get it. We do lots of training and continuously support our culture. But it's been a slow process in IT. Before I got here, culture just wasn't something people talked about it. All the training focused on the technical aspects of the job."

Let's say one of the stores experienced an issue with its point of sale software, the software used to ring up customer transactions, track sales, and control inventory. It's critical to that store's operations. If the company's IT department lacks a customer-focused culture, the IT employees might not prioritize helping a store manager work through the problem while trying to minimize the impact it has on customers.

Some companies inadvertently train their employees to actually work against their desired culture. Remember the Comcast Retention Specialists we profiled in Chapter 2? The focus of their job was to talk customers out of canceling their accounts. These Retention Specialists received extensive training on overcoming customer objections while making it difficult for customers to get what they wanted.

How to Train Employees to Embody Your Culture

A basic training program should contain three elements: objectives, instruction, and reinforcement.

Objectives represent what you want employees to know or be able to do as a result of the training. *Instruction* consists of the training activities you use to make sure employees can accomplish the objectives. And *reinforcement* is what you offer to ensure that employees don't forget what they have learned.

Here's a step-by-step guide you can use to develop a training program in your company, department, or team.

Step One: Create Objectives

The first step in developing a basic training program is to create objectives. Good training begins with clear objectives that spell out what knowledge, skills, or abilities an employee should possess by the end of the program. This allows you to measure whether that employee has met the objectives.

Training without objectives is vague, non-specific, and difficult to measure. A company might design a training program to "help employees understand our culture." But what does that mean? How will you know whether or not employees actually understand the culture?

A training program to prepare your employees to embody your customer service culture training program should start with this objective:

Employees will be able to correctly answer these questions about our customer service
vision:

* *What is our customer service vision?*
* *What does it mean?*
* *How do I personally contribute?*

Objectives like this influence how you design your training program. At a minimum, your training will need to help employees memorize your company's customer service vision, understand it well enough to explain it clearly, and link the vision to their own job duties. Employees should also be able to give specific examples of how they can embody the customer service vision on the job.

Of course, you'll need to answer these questions yourself before trying to train employees to answer them. Otherwise, it would be like giving students a test without having an answer key to grade their work.

Let's go back to Clio for a moment. The example I shared at the beginning of this chapter provided evidence that the company's support agent could answer all three questions about the customer service vision: *Our goal is to help our customers succeed and realize the full value of our Product. This results in Evangelists and less Churn.*

First, the support agent had a card on his desk with Clio's customer service vision on it, which he referenced while serving his customer. This indicated he knew the company's vision.

Second, the agent showed that he understood what the service vision meant when he told the customer he didn't want her to cancel her account and was committed to finding a solution that would work for her. This made the customer happy because she felt that he had listened to her concerns.

And finally, the support agent showed that he knew how he could personally contribute when he took the time to listen to the customer and let her know he understood her real needs. After the call, he pointed to the interaction and explained that it was his job to help customers so they remained happy and loyal Clio customers.

The last question—*How do I personally contribute?*—is sometimes difficult for employees to answer if they don't have direct contact with their customers. For example, a software developer at Clio might be tempted to think there's little she can do to provide outstanding service. However, after receiving training, that developer should realize there are actually many ways she can contribute. She can develop new features that solve pressing customer needs. She can tap into her empathy for customers to design software that's intuitive and easy for them to use. And she can be responsive to the support team when they have questions about a new feature or point out a bug that needs to be fixed.

All these actions enable Clio to deliver the kind of outstanding service that makes customers loyal to Clio and enthusiastic about recommending the software to other lawyers.

You can add other objectives to your customer service culture training program, as long as they help employees understand and embody the culture. For instance, this could be an ideal time to introduce employees to customer service standards or procedures. You might also develop different objectives for new hires than those for your experienced employees. New hires truly need an introduction to your company's culture, while experienced employees should already have an understanding of the culture and may just need to polish their skills or acquire some more advanced techniques.

Step Two: Design an Instructional Plan

The second step to developing a training program is to design an instructional plan. This plan helps your employees achieve the objectives you've written for your culture training. You'll want to create a plan that ensures every employee can provide examples of ways they personally fulfill the company's customer service vision in their daily jobs.

In their book *Telling Ain't Training*, workplace learning and performance experts Harold D. Stolovitch and Erica J. Keeps outline a simple five-step model that can easily be used to design your culture training program.[45]

1. *Rationale:* Discuss why the training is needed.
2. *Objectives:* Share the training objectives.
3. *Activities:* Conduct activities to help participants learn.
4. *Evaluation:* Determine whether the objectives have been met.
5. *Feedback:* Confirm that objectives have been met and/or coach employees to improve.

Figure 8.1 illustrates a sample customer service vision training plan for Clio's support team. You can also download a training plan worksheet at www.servicebookbook.com/tools.

Figure 8.1: Customer Service Vision Training Plan

Company: Clio
Department: Customer Support
Rationale: The purpose of this training is to help Customer Support team members understand the customer service vision and apply it to their daily work.
Objectives: Employees will be able to correctly answer these questions about our customer service vision:

* *What is our customer service vision?*
* *What does it mean?*
* *How do I personally contribute?*

Activities:

* Self-study: Ask participants to identify places where they see the customer service vision written and bring a list with them to the workshop. (Example: signs hung at workstations.)

- In class: Have participants take turns describing the customer service vision in their own words.
- Follow-up: Ask each participant to write a Thank You letter to themselves from an imaginary customer, thanking them for service that aligned with the vision. Encourage participants to attempt to earn similar feedback from a real customer.

Evaluation:

- Self-study: Verify each participant identifies at least one written example of the vision.
- In-class: Verify each participant describes the vision from their own perspective.
- Follow-up: Verify each participant writes a Thank You letter that aligns with the vision.

Feedback:

- Provide each participant with feedback on the outcome of their activities evaluations.

Activities, the third step, is where many people get stuck. Here's what I've learned in over 25 years as a corporate trainer: *keep it simple*. Many novice trainers get so excited about adding engaging or creative elements that they lose sight of the end goal, which is to make sure employees can accomplish the learning objectives.

The definition of a good training program is one that accomplishes its objectives on time and on budget. With that in mind, I prefer to follow a straightforward, three-step model for creating training activities: *tell*, *show*, and *do*.

- Tell the participants what you want them to know.
- Show them an example.
- Have the participants do something that demonstrates their new knowledge, skill, or ability.

There are many simple, creative activities you can develop following this model. Here are three examples:

This simple activity is ideal for one-on-one or on-the-job training:

* *Tell:* Explain the customer service vision.
* *Show:* Give the participant(s) a visual aid with the vision written on it.
* *Do:* Ask the employee(s) to describe how they see the vision guiding their work.

Another activity involves exploring an internal or external web page your company has that describes your organizational culture:

* *Tell:* Walk participants through the web page.
* *Show:* Point out the customer service vision and anything else that helps explain the culture (video, employee testimonials, etc.).
* *Do:* Give participants some time to explore the web page, and then follow up by asking each one to describe how he or she thinks the customer service vision relates to his or her job.

Yet another activity is a photo scavenger hunt; this works well in environments where there's ample visual evidence of the customer service vision:

* *Tell:* Discuss the company's customer service vision with participants. Then explain that you're going to send them on a scavenger hunt; their goal is to use their smart phones to take pictures related to the vision. Give them a short but workable time frame in which to do this.
* *Show:* Provide an example, such as a picture of a poster with the customer service vision printed on it, so participants know what to look for.
* *Do:* Have participants complete the scavenger hunt. As a bonus, divide them into teams and have each team give a short presentation on what they found, using their pictures as visuals. (*Optional:* Provide a list of items for participants to photograph.)

The activities you create are only limited by your budget, allotted time, and imagination. Just remember to keep it simple. Your training is effective as long as it accomplishes your objectives.

STEP THREE: PROVIDE REINFORCEMENT

This third and final step in developing a basic training program is perhaps the most overlooked part of the training process. You must continuously reinforce the concepts taught if you want the participants to remember them and regularly apply them to their work.

Customer-focused organizations have made reinforcement part of their operating DNA. As we discussed in Chapter 5, companies with strong customer service cultures align key components of their operations (goals, hiring, training, empowerment, and management) with their customer service vision. Each of these components naturally reinforces employees' knowledge and understanding of the company's service vision on a daily basis. Nevertheless, it's still a good idea to have a specific plan in place to reinforce your culture training and ensure employees are constantly reminded of the concepts they've learned.

One way to construct your plan is to use the 70-20-10 Rule, originally created by the Center for Creative Leadership.[46]

Over time, leadership development experts at the Center noticed that leaders developed their skills from three primary sources:

- 70 percent came from challenging assignments
- 20 percent came from mentors (usually the boss)
- 10 percent came from formal learning

While there's little evidence to support 70-20-10 as a hard and fast rule for leadership development, it's proven to be a useful guide for structuring training programs. Let's see how we can use it to reinforce culture training.

- *Challenging Assignments (70%)*. Clio's "Know Our Customer" initiative is an excellent example. Employees had to make time to get to know at least one customer, so they could better understand how customers used their software. Another example comes from Cars. com, where Heather Rattin and her team spend time each day solving problems that cause customer dissatisfaction.

- *Mentors (20%).* Organizational leaders should be the first people to attend customer service culture training. They need to know exactly what their employees are being taught, so they can reinforce those lessons through daily informal interactions, team meetings, department announcements (emails, etc.), and formal one-on-one feedback sessions. (We'll discuss more ways for leaders to reinforce the customer service vision in Chapter 10.)

- *Formal Learning (10%).* This might include a training class, e-learning program, one-on-one session, or other learning event used to initially train employees on how to embody the customer service culture. Customer-focused organizations like Clio and JetBlue make sure all new employees receive extensive training on the company culture. They also provide periodic refresher training to ensure employees don't stagnate.

Providing employees with constant training on the culture may seem like a lot of work—and it is. The effort is well worth it.

Let's go back to the Clio support agent whose story we shared at the start of this chapter. What would have happened if he had not been trained to embody Clio's customer service vision? The customer might have grown frustrated and asked to speak to a supervisor, which would take up valuable time that the supervisor could otherwise have spent coaching and training employees. And in the end, the client might have cancelled her account since she couldn't get what she wanted, which would cost Clio years of reliable revenue and any potential referrals she would have made to other law firms.

Now, multiply that by the dozens of interactions that single support rep has with customers each day. Multiply that number again by the 20 agents on the team. In just one day, there could be hundreds of customers who are impacted, for better or worse, by employees' ability to embody the culture.

Fortunately, the support agent was well trained. He was enthusiastic about Clio's culture and demonstrated a genuine desire to help his customer succeed. She ended the call happy with her service and determined to keep her account. And that made all that training worthwhile.

NOTES:

45 Harold D. Stolovitch and Erica J. Keeps, *Telling Ain't Training,* (Alexandria, VA: ASTD Press, 2002).

46 Ron Rabin, "Blended Learning for Leadership: The CCL Approach," *Center for Creative Leadership*, 2014. http://insights.ccl.org/wp-content/uploads/2015/04/BlendedLearning Leadership.pdf

CHAPTER 9

Empowering Employees to Support Your Culture

● ● ●

KANYON HILLAIRE UNDERSTANDS THAT MAKING customers feel confident goes a long way toward their having a good experience. He's a Safelite AutoGlass technician who fixes and replaces broken glass—cracked windows, dinged windshields—on cars.

It's annoying for a customer to experience a broken car window. On top of that, it can be unsettling to have a stranger arrive at your home or business and ask for the keys to your car.

Hillaire understands he needs to quickly build rapport with his customers. "Trust is a very big thing," explained Hillaire. "It takes years and years to trust somebody, and we have minutes."[47]

On a normal service call, Hillaire builds trust by carefully explaining the procedure before he starts working. However, one day he went to call a customer to confirm his arrival time and discovered that this customer was deaf. This meant it would be much harder to provide his normal trust-building explanation.

Hillaire decided to visit his friend Amanda, who knows American Sign Language. He recorded a video on his cell phone of Amanda signing Hillaire's explanation of the service process. The video began with, "My name is Amanda. My friend, Kanyon, asked me to help him explain how today's appointment will go." When Hillaire went on his service call, he showed his customer the video, and it immediately broke the ice.

This simple gesture wasn't in a Safelite AutoGlass employee training manual. It was something Hillaire did on his own initiative. He didn't ask for permission to record the video or to spend the extra time. He just did it.

I asked Hillaire why he didn't write down the instructions, instead of taking all that time to meet his friend and create the video. Hillaire explained that his goal was bigger than just providing information.

"Customer service for me is allowing that person to feel comfortable and safe. Then they can trust me, and when I am working on their car or truck, they want to trust me. So yes, I could have written it down, but I would have missed out on the joy I saw in my customer's face as he was watching that video. I would have missed out on watching the walls drop and watching the trust begin to grow."

Stories like this have helped Safelite AutoGlass develop a reputation for outstanding customer service. The company's service has been profiled in books, blogs, and podcasts. In 2016, Safelite won two awards from the insurer USAA for innovation and supplier excellence in contributing to USAA's own outstanding service reputation. This is a big deal, especially when you consider that USAA is regularly ranked as the number one customer service company in the United States.[48]

Like the other companies profiled in this book, Safelite has worked hard to develop a customer-focused culture. Safelite calls it *People powered, customer driven.* One of the keys to its success is empowering employees like Hillaire to deliver exceptional service.

How Safelite Empowers Employees to Deliver Outstanding Customer Service

Some people think of empowerment as the ability to go above and beyond the call of duty. Hillaire's choice—to go out of his way to make a connection and build trust with a deaf customer—is a perfect example of this.

But empowerment means much more. Empowerment is putting employees in a position where it's easy for them to provide outstanding customer service.

Many customer service leaders have told me that the number-one obstacle to empowerment is getting employees to realize how much they're really able to do for their customers. Employees must possess a strong desire to proactively look for opportunities to deliver outstanding customer service. So empowerment starts with employees having a service mindset.

Safelite's customer service vision provides employees with clear guidance on what they're expected to do:

Achieve extraordinary results by looking at our business through the eyes of our customers and making it easy for them to do business with us and ensuring their experience is memorable.

Hillaire used the vision as a guide when serving his customer. He started with a desire to make the customer feel comfortable, so he tried to imagine the service call from the customer's perspective—i.e., *through the eyes of the customer.* Hillaire knew the video of his friend Amanda signing his explanation of the procedure would make it easier for the customer to understand the process. By taking the time to create a personal video, he ensured the customer's experience was memorable.

This service mindset starts at the top. Tom Feeney, the company's CEO, described the empathy technicians are expected to display for customers who need glass repaired on their vehicles. "There's a lot of emotion going through your mind. What we try to do is bring a peace of mind to that experience."[49]

But this service mindset is just the starting point for empowerment because empowering employees means providing them with the resources, tools, and authority to serve customers at a high level. Safelite uses its customer service vision to guide the development of processes that enable employees to succeed.

Consider a typical service appointment. A customer connects with Safelite either directly or through their insurance company. When they call, the customer is immediately connected to a live person rather than being routed through an annoying phone menu. Within a few minutes, the Safelite customer service rep is able to diagnose the problem, identify the part needed to fix it, check inventory to make sure the part is in stock, confirm what's covered under the customer's auto insurance policy, and schedule a technician to come do the repair. Customers can also choose a self-service option on the Safelite website that guides them through this process.

Most customers don't realize how much planning and how many resources are required to deliver this kind of service. Safelite has to staff its contact center with enough people to answer each phone call with a live person. Employees need to be trained to ask the right questions to determine what work needs to be done. The company has to have a robust computer system capable of checking inventory, connecting with various insurance companies, and managing technician schedules.

This customer-focused approach continues on to the service call itself. On the day of their appointment, customers receive an email with a picture of the technician who will be visiting them, including a brief biography. Technicians also call or text customers directly to let them know they're on their way to the appointment. Once they arrive, technicians must have the skills to develop rapport with customers and then expertly complete the repair.

The entire repair process is designed to make it easy for technicians to serve their customers and fulfill the customer service vision. Emailing customers a picture and biography of their technician ahead of time to make them feel more confident is an example of *looking at our business through the eyes of our customers.* Allowing customers to quickly schedule an appointment and have the technician come to them (versus driving to a service center) is part of *making it easy for them to do business with us.* And a unique part of the Safelite process means that the technician will vacuum the customer's car and clean all the windows (not just the new one) as part of the service—which is a powerful way of *ensuring their experience is memorable.*

All this combines to help Safelite *achieve extraordinary results.*

Having a good product or service backed by the appropriate resources, tools, and processes can empower employees to deliver excellent customer service most of the time. However, there are still occasions when something unusual happens, and an employee needs to be able to depart from the normal routine. A procedure can't be created for every possible situation, but employees can be encouraged to use the customer service vision as a compass to point them in the right direction.

Let's go back to Kanyon Hillaire. Safelite technicians like Hillaire are trained to look for ways to connect with their customers and develop rapport.

Shooting a video of his friend explaining the service procedure in American Sign Language is an example of using that training (and Hillaire's own natural instincts) to find a way to connect with a deaf customer.

Customer-focused companies like Safelite also empower their employees to help the company continuously improve. After his service call, Hillaire emailed Renee Cacchillo, the Vice President for Customer Experience and Brand Strategy, to share his story and suggest that a video like his be created for all technicians to use.

That in itself is extraordinary. Safelite has over 11,000 employees, yet Hillaire felt comfortable reaching out to a senior leader. That would be unthinkable in many large companies, where frontline employees jokingly refer to the corporate office as "the ivory tower" and often don't even know the names of key executives.

It was also extraordinary that Cacchillo listened to Hillaire's feedback. Like many effective leaders, she knows that great ideas can come from people doing the daily work. Hillaire's suggestion made so much sense that Safelite now equips its technicians with videos explaining the service procedure in both American Sign Language and Spanish.

Trusting employees to do the right thing is another essential element of empowerment. Each service appointment involves a one-on-one connection between a customer and a Safelite employee. That requires the company to trust people like Hillaire to follow company procedures and use good judgment with limited supervision.

Like other customer-focused companies, Safelite emphasizes hiring the right people and then giving them adequate training to understand and embody the company culture. They also understand that employees naturally tend to be trustworthy if they've bought into the culture and are empowered to serve their customers.

Another terrific example came from Bright House Networks. It provided cable, internet, telephone, and home security service to approximately 2.5 million customers spread out over five states, before the company was purchased by Charter Communications in 2016. Bright House Networks' customer service agents were empowered to issue a customer account credit of up to $1,000 without seeking permission from a supervisor.

The company had a process where any credit of $250 or higher was reviewed by a supervisor. The credit had already been issued by the time of the review, so it was purely intended to ensure that customer service agents were making good decisions. If an agent made a questionable call, their supervisor could coach them on how to make a better choice in the future.

During the first year the policy was in place, managers didn't find a single credit that was issued inappropriately. The lesson here is that the customer service agents saved their customers and their company time and aggravation by issuing credits that supervisors would have eventually issued anyway.

Empowerment is a major reason for the success of many customer-focused companies. Clio avoids scripts and encourages customer service agents to use their own personalities when interacting with customers. REI has a generous returns policy that enables associates to accept most returns without any hassle. And you'll recall that Shake Shack's CEO, Randy Garutti, challenged employees at a new store to "put us out of business because you are so damn generous with what you give the people who walk in this door."

WHAT CAN HAPPEN IF YOU DON'T EMPOWER YOUR EMPLOYEES

Employees who aren't empowered often find themselves in situations where pleasing customers seems impossible. They might miss opportunities to go above and beyond because the company culture doesn't encourage them to think outside of standard procedures. Or they might feel victimized by a poor product, a broken process, or an overly restrictive policy that makes it hard for them to do their job.

One such occasion happened when a winter storm tested employee empowerment at a hotel in a small town in West Texas. The storm had shut down the highway east of town. This meant that guests who were scheduled to check out and drive east extended their stay for another night. Still other travelers heading east stopped their trip short, since this was the last town before the roads were closed. The hotel quickly sold out at what was normally a quiet time of year.

The lone hotel clerk working the front desk was overwhelmed. Guest after guest arrived without a reservation, but she had to turn them away because the hotel was out of rooms. To make matters worse, the hotel's computer system went down, which meant the clerk had to manage the check-in process manually.

This caused a problem when a couple with a reservation tried to check in, only to find their room was already occupied. The hotel clerk panicked. She had miscounted the rooms where guests had extended their stay, and now she wasn't sure which rooms were occupied and which ones were not. She tried to assign them to another room, but that one, too, was occupied.

It was late and the tired couple was getting frustrated. Meanwhile, there was a growing line of arriving guests forming in the lobby, waiting to find out if they would have a place to stay that night. It was so overwhelming that the clerk burst into tears.

The front desk clerk struggled because she wasn't empowered. She hadn't been taught what to do when an unexpected event dramatically changed the hotel's occupancy. The computer, a tool she normally relied upon to keep track of room assignments, was down. She repeatedly called her boss for help, but her boss wasn't answering his cell phone. And the front desk clerk lacked a customer-focused mindset that would have enabled her to improvise and find a way to make the best of a bad situation.

Fortunately, a guest with hotel experience intervened. She suggested that the front desk associate look for reserved rooms where guests hadn't yet arrived. It was nearly 11pm, and some guests with reservations simply weren't going to arrive because they couldn't get past the road closures. The associate found one room that matched the criteria and was able to check the couple in after walking to the room herself to verify it was indeed unoccupied.

Operational problems like this make it hard to empower employees. As of 2016, McDonald's has spent seven straight years ranked last on the American Customer Satisfaction Index for limited service restaurants.[50] Part of the company's challenge is that its menu expanded 365 percent from 1980 to 2014. Each new menu item adds additional processes, equipment, and employee training requirements, making it challenging for thousands of company-owned and franchised McDonald's to implement updates consistently. This increases the likelihood for errors, which in turn aggravates customers. For example, a study by *QSR Magazine* found that a whopping 12 percent of McDonald's drive-through orders contain an error.[51]

A lack of empowerment also contributed to the demise of the once-popular Borders bookstore chain. The company's inventory management was so poor that sales associates would often be unable to find a product for a customer, even if that product was physically located somewhere in the store. Research conducted by Zeynep Ton from the MIT Sloan School of Management and Ananth Raman the Harvard Business School revealed that this happened in approximately one out of six customer interactions when a customer asked for helping finding an item.[52] These sales associates wanted to help the customer and make the sale, but they didn't have the ability. Remember, a key aspect of empowerment is that the employee has all the right resources available to do their job.

Contact centers also provide an excellent example of how empowerment impacts service quality. A 2015 study by Mattersight discovered that 66 percent of customers who call customer service are already frustrated by the time they get a customer service rep on the phone.[53] That's because, unlike Safelite, the typical contact center requires customers to wade through a frustrating maze of phone menus and then wait on hold before someone answers the call.

This puts the customer service rep at a disadvantage since their customer is already upset, but it often gets worse. A 2015 research report from the International Customer Management Institute revealed that 74 percent of contact centers don't fully empower their employees to deliver outstanding customer service.[54]

And that feeling of disempowerment can cause employees to give up and stop even trying to serve their customers. Technical support agents at a business-to-business software company experienced this when the company released an update to its software. The new software was confusing to the small business owners who used it, and it had several bugs that made it malfunction. This caused such a barrage of customer calls that wait times sometimes extended up to an hour.

The technical support reps felt victimized. After all, *they* didn't create the confusing software update that didn't work properly. *They* weren't responsible for staffing decisions that left the support team unable to handle the influx of calls. It felt fundamentally unfair to the support reps that they had to face the brunt of customers' anger for a problem they didn't cause and couldn't fully fix. Many members of the team started feeling hopeless and resentful and stopped providing the empathetic and thorough service they normally provided.

How to Empower Your Employees

Customer-focused companies do two things to empower their employees.

First, the company develops a culture that instills a customer-focused mindset in employees. Second, the company provides employees with the tools, resources, and authority to serve their customers at the highest level.

Previous chapters in this book helped you lay the foundation for creating a customer-focused mindset, where employees are obsessed with customer service. It starts with having a clear customer service vision, and then using that vision to point the entire company in the same direction. Employees must know the vision and understand how it relates to their work. Goals should be set in alignment with the vision, and employees should be hired and trained to deliver the type of service that the vision describes.

The second part of empowerment involves putting employees in a position to succeed. There are a few things you can do to ensure this happens:

1. Invest in resources, tools, and equipment.
2. Define standard operating procedures.
3. Give employees the right authority.

Invest in Resources, Tools, and Equipment

Safelite customers get peace of mind, in part because customer service reps have the ability to quickly schedule a service call while identifying the right part, checking for an available technician, and reviewing the customer's insurance coverage. The company had to make some big investments in systems and staffing to make this happen, but customers are more loyal because of their experience. They're more likely to tell a friend about Safelite, which leads to more business. And Safelite can serve its customers more efficiently, which saves money.

In October 2014, Bright House Networks answered just 50 percent of customer calls within 30 seconds. Recognizing that this was a problem, the company invested heavily in a new unified system enabling it to route customer calls more efficiently between its multiple contact centers, so employees could provide faster service. One year later, more than 90 percent of calls were answered within 30 seconds.

Making these sorts of investments isn't cheap; you'll need to weigh the cost of the investment against the potential gain to justify the expense. Areas to explore include revenue gain (increased customer loyalty, fewer lost sales, higher average order value, etc.), reduced servicing costs (fewer discounts for poor service), improved service efficiency (reduced cost per contact, improved first contact resolution, etc.), and improved reputation (increased word-of-mouth referrals, better ratings on review sites, etc.).

Let's say you invest $100,000 in a new computer system for your customer service team. You calculate that the new system will help your team serve customers faster and more accurately, which will result in an additional $40,000 in repeat business per year. If you divide the $100,000 expense by the $40,000 gain, you can see how long it will take for your investment to pay off:

$$\$100,000 \div \$40,000 = 2.5 \text{ years}$$

It's ultimately up to you (and your CFO, CEO, etc.) to decide if an investment is worthwhile, but this is a helpful exercise.

And you can't expect your employees to consistently deliver outstanding service if they're using outdated or non-functioning systems and tools.

Define Standard Operating Procedures

Having a standard way of doing things may seem counter to empowering employees, but it's an essential step. Remember that empowerment means enabling employees to provide outstanding customer service. Standard operating procedures help employees serve their customers consistently across the whole team. These procedures should reflect the best known way of doing things while still giving employees the flexibility to adjust to unusual circumstances.

At Safelite, it's standard procedure to email a customer a picture and bio of their technician to help build trust and confidence. The technician is then expected to personally contact the customer to confirm their arrival time. And the standard procedure calls for the technician to spend a few minutes building rapport with the customer while he or she explains the repair process.

All these standards combine to create a consistent experience, regardless of who the service technician may be. When a customer has a good experience with Safelite, they'll likely call the company a couple of years later when a rock dings their windshield again. It's important that the customer has the same great experience, even though it's likely to be a different technician who does the work. Standard operating procedures help ensure that's what happens.

It's also easier to manage employees when there's a set way of doing things. New hires can learn from clearly-documented practices that are proven to be successful. Managers can supervise their employees in a consistent manner.

Companies like Safelite have also discovered that standards can't always be created from the top down. Best practices in customer-focused companies are often identified by frontline employees. For instance, Kanyon Hillaire took the initiative to create a video for a deaf customer, but he went even further to share his idea with senior leadership. As a result, the company created videos in American Sign Language and Spanish that are now part of the standard procedure for interacting with customers whose preference is one of those languages.

One customer service leader shared a common-sense approach to setting standards and best practices. Before putting a procedure in place, he has employees test the procedure to make sure it actually works as well as intended.

Getting employee input improves employee buy-in, but it also prevents broken processes or unrealistic expectations from being implemented.

Give Employees the Right Authority

A process or procedure can't be designed for every eventuality. There are many customer service situations that are unique, unusual, or unprecedented. In other situations, it's simply more efficient to give employees the discretion to make decisions that a supervisor would make anyway. Requiring an employee to seek approval before taking a common-sense action only wastes the customer's and employee's time, and can make the employee feel inept or untrusted.

There are three keys to empowering employees with the appropriate authority to serve their customers.

The first is to develop clear red lines that cannot be crossed. The $1,000 limit for customer account credits at Bright House Networks is a good example. This means a $975 credit is up to the customer service rep's discretion, but a $1,005 credit is not allowed without permission. These red lines make it clear what employees are and are not allowed to do.

The second key is to allow employees to operate in the gray area between a standard operating procedure and a red line without fear of punishment. This is where employees must be able to use their own discretion.

Let's say a manager discovers an employee issued a $500 account credit that he disagrees with. That credit is well below the $1,000 red line, so the manager should not discipline the employee in any way for using what the employee believed to be appropriate judgment. The fastest way to disempower an employee is to give them grief for doing exactly what you previously told them they could, and even should, do.

That leads us to the third key to empowerment: coaching. If a manager disagrees with an employee's decision to issue a $500 credit, he shouldn't punish her for exercising her own judgment, but he should still engage the employee in a conversation. The goal is to understand why the employee made that decision and help the employee understand how to make a better decision in the future.

Figure 9.1 shows a sample empowerment procedure for valet parking attendants working at a hotel. You can download an empowerment procedure worksheet at www.servicecuturebook.com/tools.

Figure 9.1: Sample Empowerment Procedure

Title: *Courtesy Discount Procedure*
Purpose: Our motto is "Clean, fast, and friendly service." Valet parking attendants may use this procedure to offer hotel guests a discount anytime our service falls short of our motto.
Procedure:

1. **Identify a guest service issue.** It's better to notice something before a guest does (ex: a dirty car windshield), so you can fix it quickly. You can also use this procedure if the guest complains about our service.
2. **Resolve the issue.** You may offer the guest a courtesy discount up to the full value of the parking charge. Keep in mind that there may be other ways to resolve the issue to the guest's satisfaction. For example, a dirty windshield can be quickly cleaned.
3. **Record the discount.** After serving the guest, note the courtesy discount in the Courtesy Discount Log. Be sure to indicate the reason a discount was given.

Step number three is critical. Your manager will review all discounts and may have some follow-up questions for you. The purpose is to identify any service trends that need to be addressed. For example, five discounts for dirty windshields in two days may signal that we need to find a better way to keep our guests' windshields clean!

One big concern with empowering employees is that they'll give away too much. The opposite is frequently true. Managers often have to spend time encouraging employees to do more for customers, not less.

Another big concern is making sure employees make consistent decisions. That's where coaching comes into play. A manager who frequently discusses empowerment with employees in both an individual and team setting will help calibrate the team so they all have a similar understanding of the best way to handle certain situations.

Recall that empowering employees means putting them in a position to succeed. It's a combination of the right resources, clear standards to follow, and the authority to use their discretion. It's also imperative that leaders monitor their operations to ensure that empowerment is working.

Here's an example. A hotel advertised that its airport shuttle arrived every 20 minutes. Unfortunately, shuttles actually took closer to 30 minutes to arrive. This meant that shuttle drivers weren't empowered to meet the 20-minute promise.

Measuring how the shuttle's performance stacked up against what guests expected was a key first step, so hotel managers talked to shuttle drivers to get their input. They rode the shuttle and timed each leg of the journey to understand where time was spent. Then, through a collaborative effort between managers and shuttle drivers, new procedures were implemented. The shuttle route was adjusted to be more efficient, and additional shuttles were added during peak times. All these steps finally empowered shuttle drivers to meet the 20-minute standard.

You can do the same thing with your customer service operation. Look for opportunities to improve. Collaborate with frontline employees from various teams to identify problems and get everyone on the same page. Fix problems that prevent employees from helping their customers.

There's one last step in the empowerment process.

It's essential that customer service leaders share empowerment stories with their team. These stories spark imagination by reminding employees what can be done and help them maintain an empowerment mindset.

Safelite does an excellent job of this. Let's go back to Kanyon Hillaire, who took the initiative to create a video explaining a repair process to a deaf customer. Safelite posted a short video on YouTube and the company website detailing Hillaire's story as an example of a creative way to connect with a customer.

Examples like this inspire other employees. They reinforce the concept of employee empowerment by showing how someone used their resources, tools, and authority in a creative way. Celebrating examples such as Hillaire's also makes it safe for other employees to overcome obstacles and find a way to achieve the company's customer service vision.

NOTES:

47 You can see more of Hillaire's perspective in this YouTube video: https://www.youtube. com/watch?v=lbsyEMtUGEk.

48 Bradley Lehman, "USAA Awards Companies for Innovation, Veteran Support and More," *USAA*, June 9, 2016. https://communities.usaa.com/t5/Press-Releases/USAA-Awards-Companies-for-Innovation-Veteran-Support-and-More/ba-p/93517.

49 Tom Feeney interview with Rob Markey, "Net Promoter at the heart of a cultural transformation: How Safelite turns hassles into smiles," *Net Promoter System Podcast*, March 2015. http://www.netpromotersystemblog.com/2015/03/10/net-promoter-at-the-heart-of-a-cultural-transformation-how-safelite-turns-hassles-into-smiles/.

50 The American Customer Satisfaction Index publishes these ratings on its website: http:// theacsi.org.

51 "The Drive-Thru Performance Study: Order Accuracy," *QSR*, accessed December 21, 2016. https://www.qsrmagazine.com/content/drive-thru-performance-study-average-service-time.

52 Zeynep Ton and Ananth Raman, "The Effect of Product Variety and Inventory Levels on Misplaced Products at Retail Stores: A Longitudinal Study" (working paper), *Harvard Business School*, June 2004. http://pages.stern.nyu.edu/~gjanakir/Ton_and_Raman6-10-04. pdf.

53 "Please Hold for a Reality Check: The Real Reasons Consumers are Fed Up with Call Centers," *Mattersight*, 2015. http://www.mattersight.com/resource/please-hold-for-a-reality-check-real-reasons-consumers-are-fed-up-with-call-centers/.

54 "Own the Moments! Understanding the Customer Journey," *ICMI Research*, 2015. http:// www.icmi.com/Resources/Webinars/Own-the-Moments-2015-ICMI-Research-Findings.

CHAPTER 10

How Leadership Can Make or Break Your Culture

IN OCTOBER 2012, HURRICANE SANDY descended on New York City. Governor Andrew Cuomo ordered evacuations and declared a state of emergency.

While most New Yorkers worried about their safety or the damage caused by the storm, Anthony Casalena worried about websites.

Casalena is the CEO and founder of Squarespace, a company that makes it easy for people without programming experience to build a website. Artists, bloggers, entrepreneurs, celebrities, and many others use Squarespace because of its intuitive features, beautifully designed templates, and outstanding customer support.

The data center housing Squarespace's servers was in New York City. The hurricane knocked out the power, which normally wouldn't interrupt Squarespace's service because the building had a backup generator that could keep things going for three or four days. But then the building's basement flooded, shutting down the fuel pump that sent fuel from the basement tank to the generator on the 17th floor.

Casalena received a message from the data center telling him the generator only had 12 hours of fuel left. This meant Squarespace, and all the websites it powered, would soon go offline. Jesse Hertzberg, the company's Chief Operating Officer at the time, posted an update on Squarespace's website telling customers to expect the site to go down soon. "We will do everything in our power to get Squarespace running as soon as possible, and we will remain online for as long as it is safe."

Casalena knew he had to do something, so he hurriedly left his SoHo apartment and walked to the data center. He later explained his thought process in an interview with *The Observer.* "I am really, really proud of Squarespace's uptime and everything we accomplished. So, sitting there in an apartment where there's no electricity or anything else—I mean, I would have to be, like, so lame not to walk down to the data center and just try and help. What am I going to do, sit at home in my apartment? That's just absurd."[55]

When Casalena arrived, he realized that the generator on the 17th floor was working fine. The problem was getting fuel there to keep it running. So Casalena organized a bucket brigade to manually haul fuel to the generator. Employees from Squarespace, Peer1 (the company that hosted Squarespace's servers), and Fog Creek (Peer1's parent company) worked through the night to maintain the generator's fuel supply.

Miraculously, Squarespace managed to keep its service running, which meant that thousands of customer websites stayed online. Casalena reflected on the team's herculean efforts. "It's okay to care about things, you know? Even things as silly as websites."[56]

This was an extraordinary situation, but it was also a reflection of Squarespace's customer-focused culture. The enterprising spirit that Casalena displayed that night permeates throughout the entire company.

How Squarespace Leaders Reinforce the Culture

Casalena wasn't working alone to keep the data center running during Hurricane Sandy. He pushed the initiative and modeled the necessary commitment, but other employees were needed, too. Employees found fuel drums on craigslist that were used to haul the fuel. They manually carried the drums up to the 17th floor, which was a challenging physical task. Still more Squarespace employees were required to run normal operations. Others kept customers informed by posting frequent updates on the Squarespace status page and Twitter, and answering customer emails. A few more brought food to those working nonstop to keep the data center running.

Leadership is an essential element of creating a customer-focused culture. Leaders provide employees with direction, guidance, and inspiration, which means leaders must model the customer-focused culture. It's unlikely that Squarespace's employees would have shown this extraordinary level of commitment and dedication during a natural disaster if their CEO wasn't leading the way.

Casalena and his senior leaders consciously help employees connect with the company's customer service vision. The vision consists of Squarespace's mission statement framed by six core values. The mission is *Squarespace makes beautiful products to help people with creative ideas succeed*, and the six core values are:

- Be Your Own Customer
- Empower Individuals
- Design Is Not a Luxury
- Good Work Takes Time
- Optimize Towards Ideals
- Simplify

Casalena's hiring philosophy is a great example of how to hire people who are aligned with the mission and values. Casalena explained to the venture capital blog *First Round Review* that when you hire for culture fit, "You have people you can trust to make the best decisions without you while remaining aligned with your vision."[57] We learned about the importance of hiring for culture fit in Chapter 7, but it's Casalena's insistence that ensures Squarespace includes culture fit as a key part of its employee screening process.

A tangible example of how hiring for culture fit impacts service is the support team's ability to understand and empathize with customers. Jesse Hertzberg, Squarespace's former COO, told me, "Everyone who works here is a customer." They all have Squarespace websites of their own, whether it's a personal blog, a side business, or some other online presence, thereby fulfilling the *Be Your Own Customer* core value.

This empowers technical support agents to quickly respond to customer issues with helpful and thorough suggestions. Support agents can create a personal connection with their customers because they know what it's like to use the product.

Casalena himself models the value that every employee is a Squarespace user. He started the company in 2004, when he wanted to find an easier way to build a website. He built the original software and spent the next several years personally supporting customers who needed assistance. As the company grew and he had to build a customer support team, Casalena was careful to ensure that support employees could serve customers with the same level of empathy that he did.

Casalena and the rest of the Squarespace leadership team have made several strategic decisions that reflect the company's customer focus. In 2012, the company decided to streamline its pricing plans (part of the *Simplify* core value). The new pricing scheme meant that some existing customers who had pre-paid for a year of service were now paying more for their service than new customers. To address this inequity, Squarespace generously offered existing customers a credit for the price difference when they switched to one of the new plans.

Most companies wouldn't forego all that revenue in the name of customer goodwill, but Squarespace's leaders understood that the credits helped engender long-term customer loyalty. It also prevented the company's support team from having to field a barrage of complaints from existing users who were angry about paying more than new customers.

Another customer-focused strategic decision came when Squarespace upgraded its product from version 5 to version 6. Squarespace 6 was such a radical product redesign that Squarespace 5 customers who wanted to use it would have to completely rebuild their websites. Most software companies who upgrade their products like this give customers a grace period to make the change before they pull the plug on the old version. Squarespace decided to do things differently.

First, the company announced that they'd continue supporting Squarespace 5 indefinitely. Customers running the old version could continue to do so without having to completely rebuild their websites using Squarespace 6.

Second, the company gave every Squarespace 5 user the ability to build a new website on Squarespace 6 for no additional charge. This meant customers could experiment with the new product and rebuild their site on Squarespace 6 at their own pace. Then they could choose to make the switch, or they could stick with their existing Squarespace 5 site.

The decision to run two versions of Squarespace simultaneously reflected a strong customer focus. Leaders like Casalena had an intimate understanding of what it's like to build and run a website, and how much hassle it is to have to re-build an existing site. They wanted to give their customers all the upside of the new product without the downside of being forced to make the switch.

Throughout this book, we've seen other leaders reinforce the customer-focused culture in their organizations.

Rob La Gesse at Rackspace reinforced the ideal of being available to customers by publishing his personal contact information in a blog post, so perhaps it was no surprise when support reps tweeted their personal numbers to customers when the phone system was down. (Taking a page out of La Gesse's book, my phone number is 619-955-7946 and my email is jeff@toistersolutions.com.)

Jerry Stritzke, REI's CEO, decided to close all REI stores on Black Friday in 2015, the busiest retail shopping day of the year. Instead, REI created a marketing campaign called #OptOutside to encourage REI employees and customers to spend time outdoors. This might have hurt short-term profits, but it was squarely aligned with REI's mission of helping people enjoy the outdoors. It sent a clear message that Stritzke truly believed in the company's customer focus.

Recall Kanyon Hillaire, the Safelite AutoGlass technician introduced in Chapter 9, who took the initiative to make a video that explained the windshield replacement procedure in American Sign Language for a deaf customer. He shared his idea with Renee Cacchillo, Safelite AutoGlass's Vice President for Customer Experience and Brand Strategy, who made a similar video available to all Safelite technicians. Cacchillo reinforced Hillaire's decision-making, so it felt safe for Hillaire and other technicians to take similar customer-focused initiatives in the future.

Leaders in customer-focused companies realize that employees look to them to set a positive example. They model the culture in their daily activities, so people understand that any executive pronouncements about culture are more than just lip service. They make strategic decisions using the culture as a guide, even when it means sacrificing short-term profits in favor of long-term customer relationships.

What Can Happen if Leaders Don't Reinforce the Culture

Many companies would have you believe that they're customer-focused even when they're not. Senior leaders extol the virtues of their unique and special culture in corporate communications and create lofty slogans to inspire employees. Meanwhile, these leaders often undermine attempts at true customer focus.

Wells Fargo, one of the largest banks in the U.S., provides a cautionary tale. In 2016, the bank was fined $185 million after it was discovered that employees had opened more than two million phony bank and credit card accounts over a five-year period. The accounts were opened in the names of existing customers—by bank employees struggling to achieve aggressive sales targets—without the knowledge or consent of those customers.

John Stumpf, the bank's CEO, had publicly championed the notion of Wells Fargo's customer-focused culture. He was quoted on the Wells Fargo website as saying, "Everything we do is built on trust. It doesn't happen with one transaction, in one day on the job or in one quarter. It's earned relationship by relationship." Even his message to employees announcing the fines for the widespread fraud maintained that the company was still customer-focused. "Our entire culture is centered around doing what is right for our customers."[58]

The reality was very different. Employees were encouraged by bank leaders to ignore the needs of their customers and do anything they could to open new accounts, even if it meant committing fraud. "I had managers in my face yelling at me," said Sabrina Bertrand, a former Wells Fargo banker. "They wanted you to open up dual checking accounts for people who couldn't even manage their original checking account."[59]

Wells Fargo's example proves that executive pronouncements about culture are meaningless if they don't match what leaders and employees are actually doing. The intense pressure to open unauthorized customer accounts overrode any notion of "doing what's right for our customers." The company's real culture was pressure-driven and deceitful.

Even seemingly small decisions can send a symbolic message to employees. One vice president at another company undermined her organization's customer-focused culture initiative when she refused to let a manager discipline or fire an employee who consistently provided poor customer service. The employee's productivity numbers were so good that they elevated the rest of the team's, and the vice president was scared that letting the employee go would reflect poorly on her business unit's results. Allowing an employee to be misaligned with the culture, and preventing the employee's manager from addressing it, sent a clear message that this senior leader favored short-term productivity over long-term customer relationships.

Some leaders are afraid to publicly demonstrate their commitment to the culture. One company president was so uncomfortable interacting with frontline employees and customers that he went to great lengths to avoid both groups. When he made site visits to the company's various locations, he quickly sequestered himself in an office with that location's general manager while completely ignoring other employees. This president's aloofness sent the message that he considered himself too important to speak to frontline employees, which undermined his desire for employees to provide warm and friendly service.

Another challenge faced by executive leaders is relying too much on data to manage the business without having a firm grasp of what's really happening. For example, a retail store received its weekly stock shipment on Saturday mornings. Corporate leaders scheduled the stock truck to optimize the truck's routing without considering how the timing of a shipment affected the store's operations. This was the busiest sales time of the week, but the store manager wasn't allowed to add extra staff to handle stock duties plus the heavy sales-floor activity.

Corporate leaders had set a strict limit on the number of employees who could work the Saturday shift, based on historical sales data—but without taking into account increased sales that could be gained by adding sales staff during the Saturday morning rush. The store manager shared these insights with his boss, the chain's area manager, and explained how a few changes could dramatically improve sales. But the company's senior leaders stuck to their plan, despite the store manager's request because they trusted their data more than they trusted the manager who had intimate knowledge of the store's operations.

It's helpful to acknowledge that leaders face enormous pressure to drive business results. They're human, like everyone else, which means that leadership decisions are often guided by the same swirl of emotions—like optimism, fear, and a longing for acceptance—that drive frontline employee behaviors. The big difference is that all eyes are on the leadership team.

Leaders can quickly undermine the customer-focused culture they hope to create if they make the wrong decision or model the wrong behavior. That's why it's critical for organizational leaders to recognize their role in reinforcing the culture, and for them to have a clear plan to fulfill that role.

How to Reinforce Your Culture with Employees

Employees look to their boss, company executives, and other "higher-ups" in an organization for leadership on the culture. In organizations with a customer-focused culture, leaders consistently act as culture champions.

There are three primary ways they do this: they model the culture themselves, they use the customer service vision to guide strategic decisions, and they consistently communicate the culture to employees.

Here's how you can incorporate each of these practices into your own leadership activities.

Model the Culture

Anthony Casalena, Squarespace's CEO, modeled the customer service vision by helping keep the data center open during Hurricane Sandy. He didn't merely dispatch a group of employees to take care of it; Casalena was there personally. His leadership demonstrated the caring and passion for customers that he expects of his employees.

As a leader, you have to show employees what customer focus looks like. Your behavior sends a strong signal to people that you're either committed to the culture (like Casalena at Squarespace), or you're not (like John Stumpf at Wells Fargo).

One of the best ways to do this is to be visible. Spend time connecting with employees, so they see your commitment to the culture. This is especially important in large organizations with many locations spread across a wide geographical area.

Shake Shack's CEO, Randy Garutti, provides an excellent example by frequently visiting Shake Shack locations to review the operation and encourage employees. Unlike the company president I mentioned earlier, he doesn't hide in a back office. When employees observe Garutti (and other executives) interacting with employees and customers in a positive way, they understand that these leaders are truly committed to the culture.

In some organizations, leaders periodically spend time directly serving customers. They might answer customer questions in the contact center, ring up purchases in a retail store, or greet guests in a hotel lobby. Employees are inspired to use the organization's customer service vision as a guide to serve customers when they see their leaders doing the same thing.

Let Your Culture Guide Strategy

Your strategic decisions must be aligned with the culture and the customer service vision if you want a customer-focused organization. All too often, leaders unconsciously undermine the culture they're trying to create by making a decision that doesn't fit the culture. This is almost always done to chase some sort of short-term financial advantage.

Wells Fargo's fake account scandal happened in part because the company's executives pushed something called the "Gr-eight" initiative. The goal was to get customers to hold an average of eight financial products at the bank. The initiative led to unrealistic sales goals and unrelenting pressure from Wells Fargo managers that encouraged employees to open fraudulent accounts. The strategic decision to push the "Gr-eight" program created a direct conflict with the "do what's right for our customers" culture that CEO John Stumpf promoted.

Customer-focused leaders frequently forgo short-term profits to reinforce the company's culture in the long term. These enlightened leaders realize that the continued business and positive word-of-mouth from loyal, happy customers more than makes up for any temporary set-backs.

You've seen a few examples so far in this book. JetBlue leaders made the strategic decision to provide all crewmembers (employees) with training on the airline's culture and business operations, since the resulting crewmember engagement far outweighs the cost of the training. Executives at Clio know the annual software user conference is more than just a marketing boondoggle; they use the event to actively seek client feedback, so they can make improvements to the product. Safelite AutoGlass's leaders made the strategic decision to have a live person answer customer calls, even though it requires extra staffing in their contact center.

One of my clients devised an ingenious tactic to get her CEO to look past short-term cost savings in favor of supporting the company culture. My client was the Vice President of Human Resources for a rapidly-growing company. She was convinced that she needed to add additional office space to accommodate the training needs of the company's expanding employee base (her internal customers), so she put together a business case for the company's CEO.

The CEO rejected the plan because she felt the cost of leasing additional office space was too high, but the vice president was undaunted. She invited the CEO to attend a new hire orientation session and say a few words to the company's new employees. When the CEO arrived, she was horrified to see the small conference room uncomfortably crowded with people, some of whom were sitting on the credenza in the back or leaning against the wall because there was nowhere for them to sit. Many of these employees had specialized skills and training and had been heavily recruited with generous compensation packages. The CEO was dismayed to see that their first impression as employees of the company was to be packed like sardines into a tiny conference room.

The CEO approved the new office space lease shortly after attending the new hire orientation. The business case wasn't nearly as compelling as seeing a situation that was clearly misaligned with the way the company wanted to treat its employees.

Communicate the Culture

Leaders in customer-focused organizations spend a lot of time communicating the culture to employees. They remind people of the customer service vision, emphasize its importance, and share inspirational stories of employees using the vision as a guide to deliver outstanding service.

Employees understand something's importance based on how often leaders talk about it. In customer-focused companies, leaders constantly talk about service. Here are just a few opportunities where you can do the same thing:

- Company-wide newsletters
- Town hall meetings
- Posters and signage
- Site visits to individual locations, departments, or teams
- Your direct reports

Repetition and alignment are key. Senior leaders should use a variety of ways to repeatedly reinforce the customer service vision and company culture. This sends a clear signal that the culture is important.

Middle managers and frontline supervisors must also align their employee communication around a similar message. Employees will remember and understand the customer service vision when it's reinforced by multiple leaders and in multiple ways. They'll quickly discard it as irrelevant to them if the CEO makes an occasional announcement about customer focus, but their direct supervisor never mentions it.

Leadership teams must have a shared understanding of the company culture so they can reinforce the culture in a consistent way with employees. I've worked with many companies where culture initiatives struggled because senior leaders all had very different ideas about what the culture entailed and never shared those ideas with each other to make sure they were all on the same page.

I recommend that company leaders quiz each other on the same three questions all employees should be able to answer about the customer service vision (from Chapter 4):

1. What is the customer service vision?
2. What does the customer service vision mean?
3. How do I personally contribute to the customer service vision?

The answers to these questions need to be consistent among your organizational leaders if you expect your employees to answer them consistently. This also means that senior leaders, like all employees, must either embrace the culture or be asked to leave. Squarespace's Anthony Casalena told *First Round Review* that leaders don't have to be in 100 percent agreement, but they do need to be closely aligned. Senior leaders who consistently disagree with the customer service vision, or who act counter to the company culture, do more harm than good. "If you think you'd have 80% disagreement with some leaders, then some people probably shouldn't be at the company."

NOTES:

55 Kelly Faircloth, "Why Did SquareSpace's CEO Haul Diesel Up 17 Flights of Stairs? Anything Less Would be 'Lame'," *Observer*, November 5, 2012. http://observer.com/2012/11/squarespace-diesel-peer1-wall-street-hurricane-sandy-data-center.

56 Ibid.

57 "How Squarespace's CEO Pivoted to Scale for Millions," *First Round Review* (blog). http://firstround.com/review/How-Squarespaces-CEO-Pivoted-to-Scale-for-Millions.

58 John Stumpf, "Perspective on Sept. 8 settlement announcement," *Wells Fargo*, September 2016. https://stories.wellsfargobank.com/perspective-todays-settlement-announcement/?cid=adv_prsrls_1609_102495.

59 Matt Egan, "Workers tell Wells Fargo horror stories," *CNNMoney*, September 9, 2016.

A Customer-Focused Example

● ● ●

NONE OF THE CUSTOMER-FOCUSED COMPANIES profiled in *The Service Culture Handbook* wanted to be in Chapter 11. It's understandable, given the connection in the United States between "Chapter 11" and bankruptcy or going out of business.

These companies are my customers because they've helped me highlight the steps necessary to develop a customer service culture. So, we'll just skip this chapter and go straight to Chapter 12.

CHAPTER 12

Making the Commitment to a Customer-Focused Culture

MOST COMPANIES FEEL PRESSURED TO provide outstanding customer service. Keeping customers happy is an important part of earning repeat business and maintaining the company's brand reputation.

But serving customers isn't always easy. Products break, processes don't always work as intended, and getting every employee on the same page is an enormous challenge.

Now imagine the pressure your company would face if your business was developing customer support software.

That's Zendesk. Its software is used by thousands of companies to serve their own customers. All the back-end stuff most of us don't think about runs through Zendesk: keeping records of customer contacts, capturing notes from customer service agents, and routing contacts from multiple channels (phone, email, chat, etc.) to the correct person. Zendesk can even send out customer service surveys to help companies generate Voice of the Customer feedback.

The company has developed a reputation for providing outstanding customer service to the companies using its software. Its customer satisfaction rating hovers around an astounding 95 percent. It's not uncommon for customer service leaders to get excited when they talk about Zendesk and gush about how the software makes it easier for their company to deliver service. More of my clients use Zendesk than any other customer support software platform.

Customer focus initially came easily for Zendesk. The company was founded in 2007 by Mikkel Svane, Morten Primdahl, and Alexander

Aghassipour. They wanted to make customer support software that was easy to use, so customer focus was a driving principle behind the company's creation. In the beginning, the three founders were closely involved with all aspects of the operation and had direct contact with their clients.

Like many startups, the real challenge was maintaining the culture as the company grew. In just seven years, Zendesk expanded from a three-person startup run out of Mikkel Svane's kitchen into a global, publicly-traded organization with customers in 150 countries and territories and more than 1,500 employees.

Zendesk executives realized the company needed a more formal approach. Accordingly, in 2014, Zendesk made a commitment to formalizing and growing its customer-focused culture.

How Zendesk Made the Commitment to Customer Focus

The initiative started with the customer support team, which Zendesk calls the Customer Advocate team. Greg Collins was hired as the Vice President of Global Customer Advocacy in 2014, just a few months after Zendesk had its initial public stock offering. The company already had a great product, passionate customers and employees, and a proven track record. Collins was brought in to help sustain and grow the culture of customer advocacy as the company grew.

"The challenge was we were growing so fast," says Collins. "It was tough to keep everyone rowing in the same direction."

The first step in making a formal commitment to customer focus was ensuring that senior leaders supported it. The initiative would start in the Customer Advocate team, but Collins wanted it to permeate throughout the entire company.

Fortunately for Collins, the idea of formalizing the company's customer service culture resonated with executives because many critical elements were already in place. Customer focus was a core reason the three founders had started the company, and Zendesk leaders were already careful about how customer service was positioned to employees. For instance, the term *advocacy* was used for customer support, meaning that support employees—known as Customer Advocates—understood that they were there to be advocates for the customers they served.

The next step was creating a customer service vision that would serve as a shared definition of outstanding service for all Customer Advocates. As we've seen throughout this book, a customer service vision is the cornerstone of a customer-focused culture. It acts as a compass to get every employee pointed in the same direction, which was exactly what Collins had been hired to do.

Collins solicited input from every member of the nearly 200-person Customer Advocate team, encouraging Customer Advocates from around the world to share and discuss ideas with each other via an online portal. The team ultimately created a set of four values unified by a vision statement, all of which were directly aligned with Zendesk's corporate mission: *to help organizations and their customers build better relationships.*

- *Serve: Putting Service in 'Customer Service'*
- *Lead: Lead by Example*
- *Innovate: Don't Fear the Banana*
- *Have Fun: Smile, Dammit*

The vision: to be the benchmark of a people-first Support Experience
Some clarification is in order to avoid confusion.

I use the term "customer service vision" to describe a shared definition of outstanding customer service. Zendesk's customer service vision includes four values and a vision statement. For the rest of this chapter, I'll use the term "customer service vision" to reflect the overall definition and "vision" to refer to the Customer Advocate team's vision statement.

Second, "Don't Fear the Banana" references a parable about a group of monkeys placed in a cage. The story is often passed off by keynote speakers as a real scientific experiment; it's not.

Five monkeys are placed in a cage with a ladder in the middle. On top of the ladder is a banana. Whenever a monkey tries to get the banana, the other monkeys are sprayed with cold water. The monkeys quickly learn to attack any monkey that tries to get the banana.

Next, one by one, the monkeys are replaced in the cage with new monkeys—who are promptly attacked by the group as soon as they go for the banana. This behavior persists in the cage even when there are no monkeys left that had been sprayed with cold water when another monkey went after the banana. The lesson is that it's easy to accept the status quo without understanding why things are done a certain way.

"Don't Fear the Banana" was already part of the Zendesk culture when the Customer Advocate team created its customer service vision. Mikkel Svane, the company's CEO, was fond of saying it when he wanted to encourage people to challenge the status quo. As part of the newly-created value statement, "Don't Fear the Banana" incorporated the existing culture into a codified value system.

A customer service vision, whether it's a set of values, a mission statement, or another type of cultural artifact, is much more powerful when it clearly reflects an organization's already-existing culture.

The third clarification has to do with the vision: *to be the benchmark of a people-first Support Experience.* This means that Advocates and customers are equally important to Zendesk. It's common for customer support teams in software companies to become overly focused on process or technology where support agents feel unempowered to serve their customers because they're constrained by tightly-scripted procedures that don't provide enough flexibility to address each customer's unique needs. The result is that customers may feel like the support agent is talking down to them and not truly empathizing with their frustration, or even worse, customers suspect the company is using automated technology to save money by preventing them from connecting with a live person. Zendesk's Customer Advocate team emphasizes a people-first philosophy to instill the idea that serving the person is more important than focusing on the technology.

"Process and technology are very valuable," says Collins. "Yet these strategies serve people."

Collins emphasizes that the values are listed in priority order and are collectively unified by the vision. This is an important point because employees can easily get confused if there are too many cultural artifacts (like values, a vision statement, a mission statement, etc.) to memorize and follow. Zendesk Customer Advocates know their number-one priority is *Putting Service in 'Customer Service,'* which means developing healthy relationships with customers by providing clear, concise, and helpful support.

Once the values and vision were created, Collins hung them on signs in every Customer Advocate office. He spent time discussing them with Customer Advocates to ensure that every person knew what they were, what they meant, and how the customer service vision should guide their daily work.

The entire process took just a few months, from gaining executive support for the culture initiative, to working with Customer Advocates to create the values and vision, to rolling out the final customer service vision to the team. Many leaders would check the project off their to-do list at this point and move on to another initiative. For Collins, the work was just beginning.

He set about incorporating the values and vision into every aspect of the Customer Advocate team's daily work. They were incorporated into new-hire training, and every new Customer Advocate gets a personal email from Collins explaining the values and vision and their importance. The values and vision are mentioned in every all-hands meeting and in one-on-one conversations with employees.

The team is also encouraged to use the values when interacting with their coworkers. For instance, Customer Advocates can recognize each other for outstanding service. The only catch is they have to mention which one of the four values they're recognizing their colleague for emulating.

Collins implemented a quarterly Advocate Satisfaction survey to help provide a barometer of how well Zendesk is creating a *people-first Support Experience* for its support agents. The survey asks, "How much do you like or dislike your current job at Zendesk?" The results are boldly shared on a website where the current Agent Satisfaction Score is 91.5 percent.[60] "I believe that motivated, happy, and engaged Advocates is how you get motivated, happy, and engaged Customers," says Collins.

Customer Advocates now review feedback from customer satisfaction surveys on a daily basis. Positive surveys are celebrated, while negative feedback is dissected to identify opportunities for the team to improve. All this feedback is shared with the rest of the company to help other departments understand where they can contribute to increasing customer satisfaction.

Collins has invited people from other parts of the company to share in the Customer Advocate team's vision. The company has a Support Experience Program, where people from other departments can spend time working with Customer Advocates to resolve customer issues. The intent is to help employees develop customer empathy, so they can understand how their work impacts Zendesk's customers.

Irina Blok, a Zendesk product designer, described her participation in the Support Experience Program as a new employee. "Before this experience, I thought it would be easy to be an advocate. But it's a very hard job. Not only do you have to know the product completely, you have to be a people-person."

Blok continued, "Not only did I get to learn about the Zendesk product, I developed hands-on knowledge of what Zendesk is built on: helping customers solve problems."[61]

Two things really stand out about Zendesk's story. The first is that this wasn't a one-time project. Collins makes it clear that aligning all Customer Advocates around a shared customer service vision is a way of doing business. This is a true long-term commitment to building, growing, and sustaining a customer-focused culture.

The second thing that stands out is that the steps Collins took to formalize the Customer Advocate team's culture are remarkably similar to what other companies profiled in this book have done. I didn't ask Collins a set of predetermined interview questions designed to elicit responses that fit my model. We just talked. And the more he talked, the more I heard similarities with other customer-focused companies.

Collins started by getting support from his executive leadership team. Senior leaders champion the company culture in every customer-focused company profiled in this book. You can't get employees to commit to something that senior leaders won't commit to themselves.

The next step was developing a customer service vision. Every customer-focused company profiled in this book has one. They all look different, but every one of them provides a clear definition of outstanding customer service for employees to follow.

The third piece is aligning daily work around that vision. Goals, hiring, training, processes, and leadership are all focused on delivering outstanding customer service. Progress is reviewed relentlessly, and employees soon come to realize that this is the most important aspect of their jobs. This is when they become obsessed with service.

Making a commitment like this isn't a short-term project. Collins continues to work on culture two years after he joined Zendesk. Clio, the software company you met in Chapter 8, started its culture initiative in 2013 and continues to diligently work on it today. In 2015, REI started its #OptOutside campaign to close its stores on Black Friday and has now turned it into an annual event.

Culture requires senior leaders and their employees to be in it for the long term. It's incredibly difficult to maintain a customer-focused culture without this true commitment.

What Can Happen if You Don't Commit to Customer Focus

Many leaders follow what employees jokingly refer to as a "flavor of the month" plan. A new initiative is introduced, project teams are formed, everyone spends a lot of time on it, and then it just goes away. Soon, another new initiative takes its place. People are always working on something new, but nothing seems to stick.

One company wanted to develop a customer-focused culture, but senior leaders weren't willing to make a full commitment. The first year, the company president approved an initiative to create a customer service vision, but then quickly stopped the initiative in order to refocus her leadership team on cost-cutting in an effort to improve year-end profits. A few months later, the president was fired by the company's ownership group, in part because the company was delivering poor service.

A new president was hired and expressed his commitment to restarting the culture initiative. First, though, he wanted to focus the company on employee engagement, not realizing that culture and engagement go hand-in-hand. The company ran through the same process that many companies use: conducting an employee satisfaction survey, forming committees to review the results, and then ultimately doing very little to make improvements.

The next year, the president expressed interest in the culture initiative, but held off to focus on customer experience. He took the same approach as the employee engagement initiative: a one-time survey was conducted, committees were formed, and nothing really happened.

Once again, the president missed the connection between culture, employee engagement, and customer experience. He could have been doing all three at the same time! Unfortunately, these flavor of the month initiatives gained very little traction, and very little changed because there was no real commitment. By now, the original culture ideas had been forgotten.

A major reason this company struggled was because neither president fully committed to any initiative that would fundamentally change how the organization operated. They wasted inordinate amounts of employee time and spent large sums of money on consultants to start new projects, but the promised benefits never materialized because they didn't stick with it.

Some leaders try to make customer focus an initiative just for frontline employees. As we learned in Chapter 10, this approach doesn't work either. Employees follow the example set by their leaders. This means leaders need to model the culture themselves, use the culture to guide strategic decision-making, and consistently communicate the culture to employees.

One customer service executive lamented that she wanted to build a customer-focused culture, but her company's CEO "didn't go for that touchy-feely stuff." The harsh reality is that a culture initiative can only go as high as the most senior person supporting it. She realized that she wouldn't be able to get the entire company to focus on service until the CEO made it a priority, but she also understood that she could have a positive impact on areas she controlled directly. So she set out to develop a customer-focused culture among the people who reported to her.

Impatience can also sink a customer-focus initiative, because executives often severely underestimate the time and effort required to change a company culture. It seems like every year a research firm produces a survey that shows customer focus is a top priority for corporate executives, only to replace that prediction with a similar one the next year.

For instance, a 2013 study by the research arm of the computer networking firm Oracle revealed that 93 percent of senior executives felt improving customer experience was a top priority for 2014.[62] A study released in February 2015 by Oracle and Forbes Insights, the research group for *Forbes* magazine, showed that 88 percent of customer service executives felt their organizations were making good progress toward meeting the needs of their customers.[63] Meanwhile, the American Customer Satisfaction Index declined for eight straight quarters during this same time period, from Q1 2014 to Q4 2015.[64]

One organization wanted to develop its culture and began by following the steps outlined in this book. The organization's leaders developed a customer service vision, and employees in individual departments received training on what the vision meant and how they could contribute. Unfortunately, executives soon became impatient and lost focus on the initiative.

The first sign of trouble came when leaders didn't make time to support the initial implementation. Senior executives were scheduled to attend vision rollout training programs to express their support for the customer service vision, but each one found an excuse to cancel their participation. Some departments were allowed to skip the rollout training altogether because the department leader was under pressure from a senior leader to focus on other tasks. Make-up classes were promised but never materialized.

A budget freeze halted the vision rollout entirely just a few months into the initiative. The organization wanted to reallocate spending to focus on other projects that were considered higher priority than building a customer-focused culture. Meanwhile, employee morale worsened and customer satisfaction survey scores declined as employees perceived that yet another program had been started and then quickly abandoned.

Many leaders struggle to grasp the concept of true commitment. It's not something you can change with an executive announcement, a few training classes, or by hiring a team of consultants. Companies like Zendesk succeed in developing customer-focused cultures because their leaders worked for many years to include customer focus as a part of the culture. The culture initiative that Greg Collins and his team at Zendesk led simply codified and grew what was already there.

How to Commit to a Customer-Focused Culture

Take a moment to answer the following questions. These are gut-check questions, so answer them honestly. Involve other leaders if necessary, or start by taking an introspective look at your part of the organization.

Question #1: Can you identify how outstanding customer service is valuable to your business? It's not enough to say "Yes" to this question because you have a general idea of how service is important. Commitment to customer focus almost always wavers unless there's a clear understanding of how customer service directly drives business outcomes. A "Yes" to this question means you have a specific answer connecting service to financial results. Here are just a few examples:

- Can you sell more products at a higher price point, like REI?
- Can you earn loyalty from a specific customer base, like JetBlue does with leisure travelers?
- Can you generate amazing revenue per location, like Shake Shack?
- Can you become a leader in a competitive market, like Cars.com?
- Can you improve efficiency through incredible employee retention, like Publix?
- Can you decrease customer churn, like Clio?
- Can you save time and money by empowering employees, like Safelite AutoGlass?
- Can customer-focus make your products more appealing to customers, like Squarespace?

Zendesk was ready to make this change because the company needed a way to maintain its culture as it continued to grow. The market for customer service software is incredibly competitive, so the company would either gain or lose market share based on how well it served its customers.

Question #2: Are you willing to be a different leader? Shaping a culture, whether at an organizational or team level, is an incredible leadership challenge. It takes grit to stay the course when others might question you. Discipline is required to prioritize culture when it seems like a million other tasks need your attention. Humility is another important trait, since we're all human and sometimes make mistakes.

Zendesk's Greg Collins shared an impressive example about accountability. He told me that every employee is expected to speak up and say something if they see someone who isn't living the values or vision. That rule even applies to him: employees are encouraged to let him know if they think he's making a decision that's not aligned with the culture—and they do!

Question #3: Are you willing to fundamentally change the way your business operates? This is a tough test for many leaders who want to achieve customer focus but aren't ready to put in the work to make it happen. The customer-focused companies profiled in this book succeed because they do things differently than most organizations.

Some of the steps outlined in this book may represent significant changes. You'll need to use metrics differently, hire differently, train differently, give employees more empowerment than ever before, and change how leaders work with their teams. Even your strategies, tactics, and policies may need to change as you align everything around a customer service vision.

Zendesk has made core changes as its culture continues to evolve. In 2011, the company relocated its headquarters to San Francisco's Tenderloin District, a redeveloping neighborhood where companies receive tax breaks from the city in exchange for investing in the community. Mikkel Svane saw this as an opportunity to develop the company culture. "I think [moving] has helped us create a richer, more well-rounded company, where people think not just about the code, or the product we built, or the customers we serve, but also about our part in the neighborhood. I think it makes our employees smarter and better employees, and gives a meaning for their life and job."[65]

You're probably ready to make a commitment to a customer-focused culture if you can truthfully answer "Yes" to all three questions.

There's still some work to do if any of the questions is a "No" for you.

Perhaps you're not the CEO or company president. You might be wondering how to get your senior leadership on board with a culture initiative.

Unfortunately, there's no easy answer. I, too, am still searching for a secret technique that will get executives to suddenly make a full commitment to developing the right culture. But the reality is that your executives need to be able to answer "Yes" to those same three questions if you want to effect organization-wide culture change.

All is not lost if you can't make that happen. What you can do is focus on the area within your control. If you manage a contact center, then make it the most customer-focused contact center you possibly can. If you manage one location in a company that has many, then help your location develop a reputation for outstanding service. If you lead a department that provides internal service (like Human Resources, Finance, IT, Logistics, etc.), then make your department everyone's favorite go-to department in the company.

There are two things to keep in mind if you truly believe you can make the commitment to a customer-focused culture.

The first is that the process laid out in chapters 3 - 10 is a step-by-step guide. Being committed involves sticking to that process and not skipping steps.

The second thing to remember is that developing your culture takes time, and there will be bumps in the road along the way. You'll need a plan to keep everyone energized and focused.

I recommend creating an annual calendar of activities promoting the customer-focused culture to help you, your employees, and the entire organization remain focused. It's good to break this calendar down into yearly, quarterly, monthly, weekly, and daily activities. Here are some suggestions:

Yearly Activities

- Review the customer service vision to make sure it still resonates.
- Use the customer service vision as a guide during strategic planning.
- Engage employees in recommitment activities such as refresher training.

Quarterly Activities

- Hold an all-hands meeting (including your senior leadership!) to discuss the state of the business and reinforce the vision.
- Recognize employees for their contributions to the culture.
- Conduct training activities to build new customer service skills.

Monthly Activities

- Review customer-focused metrics and generate insight for improvement.
- Identify the biggest issues that hurt customer service and then solve them.
- Meet one-on-one with employees to give feedback and reinforce the customer service vision.

Weekly Activities

- Review customer feedback and generate insight for improvement.
- Hold team-level meetings to discuss top customer service priorities, resolve challenges, and reinforce the customer service vision.
- Conduct micro-trainings to reinforce one specific customer service skill. (You can use my free Customer Service Tip of the Week email for ideas. Sign-up at www.serviceculturebook.com/tools.)

Daily Activities

- Use ad hoc employee feedback opportunities to reinforce the customer service vision.
- Put out fires, and then identify and fix whatever caused the problem.
- Model the customer service vision to set an example for employees.

You can find a template to create your own customer-focused activity plan at serviceculturebook.com/tools.

Customer service leaders often ask me whether these never-ending customer-focus activities ever get stale. The answer to that is no ... and sometimes.

On an organizational level, the commitment should never waver. That's because organizations must constantly evolve to address new opportunities in the market and solve complex challenges to improve the business and serve customers even better. There's always some sort of change going on, which keeps things from getting stale.

On a team, location, or department level, customer focus shouldn't get stale, either. That's because each part of the organization must also continuously change and adapt as the organization itself evolves. New employees will join the team, and it takes work to help them learn about the culture and understand how they, too, can help promote it.

On an employee level, the relentless customer focus can get stale in certain situations. Some employees will consider their job a career and relish the opportunity to grow, so feeling stuck in the same role for years on end can feel dreary. Others will enjoy the time they spend in your organization, but it won't be part of their long-term plan, no matter how exciting you make it. The important job for a customer service leader is to ensure that all employees are committed to the culture for as long as they're there.

The companies profiled in this book maintain a customer-focused culture in part because their employees are obsessed with solving problems. They want to serve each customer better than the last one. It's a constant challenge that always presents some new wrinkle or obstacle. Employees are energized because they know the entire organization is focused on driving business results through outstanding customer service.

It's an amazing feeling to be a part of something like that. My hope is that you can use this book as a guide to create that magic in your organization.

Notes:

60 The score is periodically updated. You can view the latest results here: https://www.zendesk.com/customer-experience/customer-service/#customer-service.

61 Irina Blok, "A day in the life of a Zendesk advocate," *Zendesk* (blog), February 2016. https://www.zendesk.com/blog/day-life-zendesk-advocate.

62 Oracle, "Global Insights on Succeeding in the Customer Experience Era," 2013.

63 Jake Sorofman and Laura McLellan, "Gartner Survey Finds Importance of Customer Experience on the Rise - Marketing is on the Hook," *Gartner*, 2014.

64 The American Customer Satisfaction Index is updated quarterly. http://theacsi.org/national-economic-indicator/us-overall-customer-satisfaction.

65 Heather Somerville, "Four years after Mid-Market tax break, Zendesk wins over community," *The Mercury News*, February 20, 2015.

Index

• • •

28678818R00105

Made in the USA
Lexington, KY
21 January 2019